ALL THUMBS

Guide to
Car Care

Other All Thumbs Guides

Compact Disc Players
Home Energy Savings
Home Plumbing
Home Wiring
Painting, Wallpapering, and Stenciling
Repairing Major Home Appliances
VCRs

ALL THUMBS

Guide to
Car Care

Robert W. Wood
Illustrations by Steve Hoeft

TAB

TAB BOOKS

Blue Ridge Summit, PA

FIRST EDITION
FIRST PRINTING

©1993 by **TAB Books.**
TAB Books is a division of McGraw-Hill, Inc.

Library of Congress Cataloging-in-Publication Data

Wood, Robert W., 1933-
    An all thumbs guide to car care/by Robert W. Wood;
    illustrations by Steve Hoeft.
       p. cm.
    Includes index.
    ISBN 0-8306-4162-9 (p)
    1. Automobiles—Maintenance and repair—Amateurs' manuals.
    I. Title.
TL152.W66   1992
629.28'72—dc20   92-22801
                                        CIP

Acquisitions Editor: Kimberly Tabor
Editorial team: Susan D. Wahlman, Editor
                Joanne M. Slike, Executive Editor
                Stacey Spurlock, Indexer
Production team: Katherine G. Brown, Director
                  Wanda S. Ditch, Layout
                  Lorie White, Proofreading
                  Linda King, Proofreading
                  Tina M. Sourbier, Typesetting
Design team: Jaclyn J. Boone, Designer
              Brian Allison, Associate Designer
Cover design: Lori E. Schlosser
Cover illustration: Denny Bond, East Petersburg, Pa.
Cartoon caricature: Michael Malle, Pittsburgh, Pa.   ATS

The All Thumbs Guarantee

About the Binding

This and every All Thumbs book has a special lay-flat binding. To take full advantage of this binding, open the book to any page and run your finger along the spine, pressing down as you do so; the book will stay open at the page you've selected.

The lay-flat binding is designed to withstand constant use. Unlike regular book bindings, the spine will not weaken or crack when you press down on the spine to keep the book open.

Contents

Preface *ix*

Introduction *xi*

1 Checking the Basics *1*

2 Changing the Oil & Oil Filter *14*

3 Car Won't Start *19*

4 Car Runs Rough or Dies *44*

5 Car Overheats *58*

6 Lights *78*

7 Tires *89*

8 Air Conditioning *102*

General Troubleshooting Guide *112*

Glossary *116*

Index *124*

Preface

A collection of books about do-it-yourself maintenance and repairs, the All Thumbs series was created not for the skilled jack-of-all trades, but for the average person whose budget isn't keeping pace with today's rising costs. In earlier years, and in some areas today, families were separated from their neighbors by many miles, and they didn't have access to the variety of services now available. They had to depend on their own abilities to keep things running. Today, due to our struggling economy, many people are faced with a similar situation. The All Thumbs series can save you both time and money by showing you how to perform many common repairs or maintenance procedures yourself.

These guides cover many topics, including car care; home wiring; plumbing; painting and wallpapering; repairing major appliances; and VCR repair, to name a few. The easy-to-follow step-by-step instructions are accompanied by clear illustrations, putting the most common repairs within the ability of the average reader.

Introduction

This book is about car care, but it's not for the mechanic. It is for someone who is unfamiliar with the various systems that make up the typical car (like most of us), who depends on his or her car, and who can't afford professional help for all of the minor things that might go wrong. Today's cars have a variety of dazzling electronic features and a few thousand moving parts. However, if you understand the basics, you can often locate the problem yourself and make the repair when something goes wrong. At least you should be able to narrow the problem down to a specific area, saving a technician time (and saving you money) if you find that you do need to take your car to a professional repair shop. The purpose of this book is to introduce you to the inner workings of your car and show you how to cure its most common ailments yourself.

The first chapter provides a general description of how a car operates, and it shows how to check the oil, transmission, and brake fluids, as well as the air filter. Chapter 2 shows you how to change the oil and oil filter. The remaining chapters cover such topics as: the car won't start, the car keeps dying, the radiator overheats, electrical systems, tires, and air conditioners. Most chapters start with a troubleshooting guide and a list of the necessary tools for the job. For easy reference, the appendix is a general troubleshooting guide. For more ambitious repairs, buy a service manual for your make of car at the parts department of your local dealer or auto parts house. You can also find repair manuals at most libraries. Don't attempt any repair unless you fully understand the job. Even professionals refer to service manuals at one time or another.

Before you start any repair, read the instructions, don't be in a hurry, and work in a clean, well-ventilated area. Have clean rags or paper towels handy. Use the proper tools. For example, don't try to remove a metric nut with a standard wrench, or use pliers when a wrench is called for. Use a drop light with a cage protecting the bulb. Don't work on anything that is under warranty, or you could void the warranty. When in doubt, seek professional help.

Remember that safety always comes first. Have a first-aid kit and an ABC-type fire extinguisher handy. Never, never crawl under a car supported only by a jack. Block the wheels when changing a tire. Never completely remove a hot radiator cap. Remove any jewelry (watches, bracelets, rings, long necklaces) before making repairs. Don't wear loose clothing, ties, or scarfs, and if you have long hair, tie it back out of the way.

CHAPTER ONE

Checking the Basics

When you turn the key and start your car, an electric motor (the starter) turns the crankshaft inside the engine. Rods connected to the crankshaft move pistons up and down inside hollow cylinders. At the same time, electricity is supplied to spark plugs mounted in the top of the cylinders. A mixture of gasoline and air is drawn into the cylinders and ignited by the spark plugs. The explosion forces the pistons down, in a designed order, turning the crankshaft. A fuel pump delivers gasoline from the gas tank to the carburetor. The carburetor mixes the correct amount of air with the gas being drawn into the cylinders, and the engine runs.

When you put the car in gear, the transmission moves the power from the engine down the drive shaft to the differential (rear end). The differential transfers the power to the axle that turns the wheels. Because of the extreme heat generated by the engine, the engine temperature is stabilized by a cooling system. A 50/50 mixture of water and antifreeze flows through the engine block and draws heat from the engine into the radiator. Air flows through the radiator, cooling the mixture before it returns to the engine. When you step on the brakes, pistons inside the brake's master cylinder exert tremendous pressure on hydraulic fluid in the brake lines, forcing other pistons to apply pressure to the brake shoes or pads. The shoes press against the

1

brake drums, the pads press against rotating discs called rotors, and the car stops.

   If you listen to your car, develop a feel for it, and are alert for any unusual smells, it usually lets you know when something is wrong.

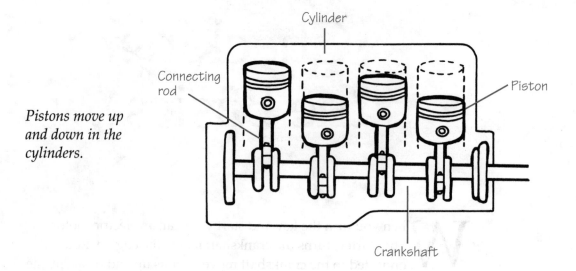

Pistons move up and down in the cylinders.

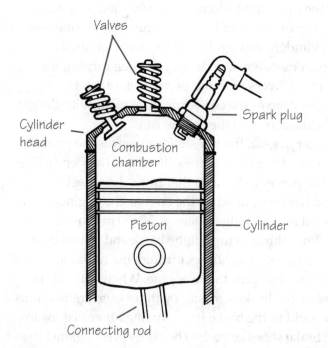

Spark plugs ignite the fuel mixture in the combustion chamber.

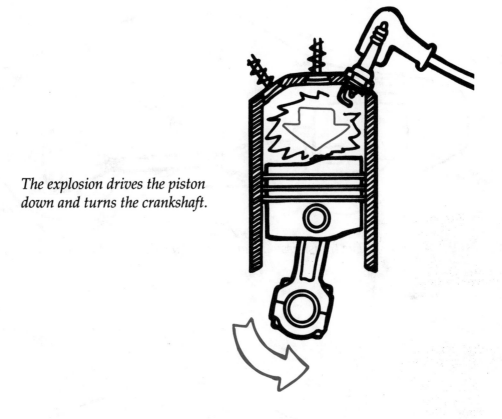

The explosion drives the piston down and turns the crankshaft.

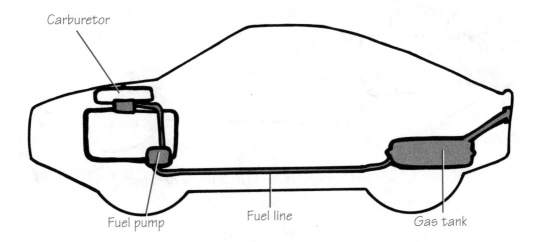

Carburetor

Fuel pump

Fuel line

Gas tank

The fuel pump delivers gasoline to the carburetor.

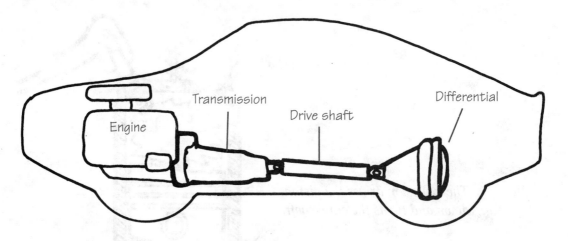

The transmission transfers engine power to the wheels.

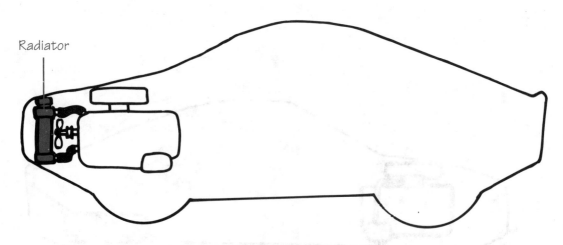

The engine coolant is held in the radiator.

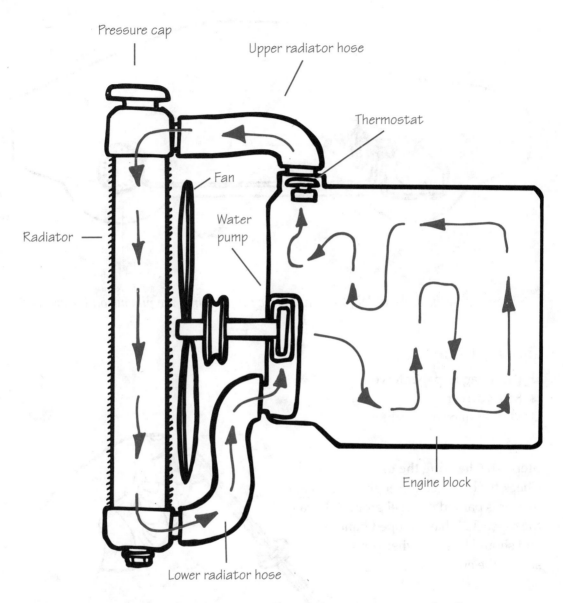

Pressure cap

Upper radiator hose

Thermostat

Fan

Water pump

Radiator

Engine block

Lower radiator hose

The water pump circulates the coolant through the engine and radiator.

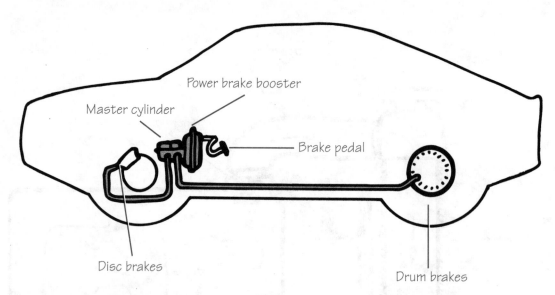

Master cylinder

Power brake booster

Brake pedal

Disc brakes

Drum brakes

Pressure on the brake pedal forces hydraulic fluid against the pistons on the brakes.

Tools & Materials

- ❏ Clean rag or paper towel
- ❏ Screwdriver
- ❏ Flashlight or droplight

Step 1-1. Checking the oil.
Check the oil when the engine is cool and
the car is parked on level ground. Locate
the dipstick. It has a looped handle
and should be somewhere on the
side of the engine.

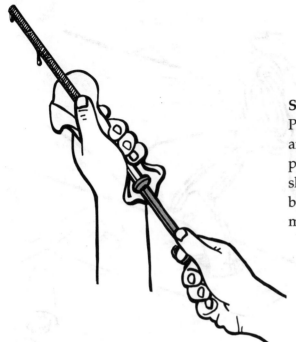

Step 1-2. Reading the dipstick.

Pull the dipstick up out of the engine and wipe the end with a clean rag or paper towel. The end is marked to show the level of the oil. The distance between the ADD mark and the FULL mark is one quart.

Step 1-3. Reading the oil level.

Insert the dipstick all the way back into the engine; then remove it. Hold the end of the dipstick horizontally against a paper towel. Clean oil is very hard to see on the stick. The paper towel will wet to the level of the oil. If the oil level is above the ADD mark, do not add any oil. If you overfill the engine, the oil could foam and damage the engine.

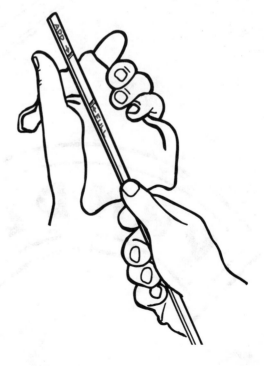

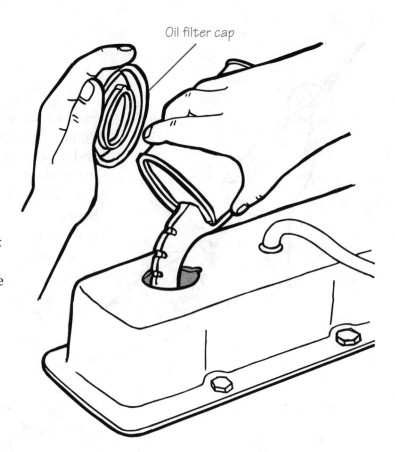

Oil filter cap

Step 1-4.
Adding oil.
If the oil level is at or below the ADD mark, remove the oil filler cap and add one quart of oil. If you don't see any oil at all, recheck. If you still don't see any oil, add one quart and check again. Continue to check and add oil until the level is above the ADD mark.

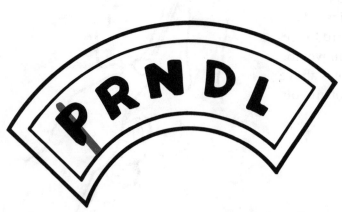

Step 1-5.
Checking the transmission fluid.
Drive the car for a few minutes to bring the transmission fluid up to operating temperature. Park the car on level ground. Leave the engine running at idle and put the transmission in PARK. Set the parking brake.

Step 1-6.
Locating the
transmission dipstick.
The transmission dipstick is probably between the engine and the firewall. Remove the dipstick and wipe the end with a clean rag. Reinsert the dipstick all the way. Remove it again and check the fluid level. It should be between the ADD and FULL marks.

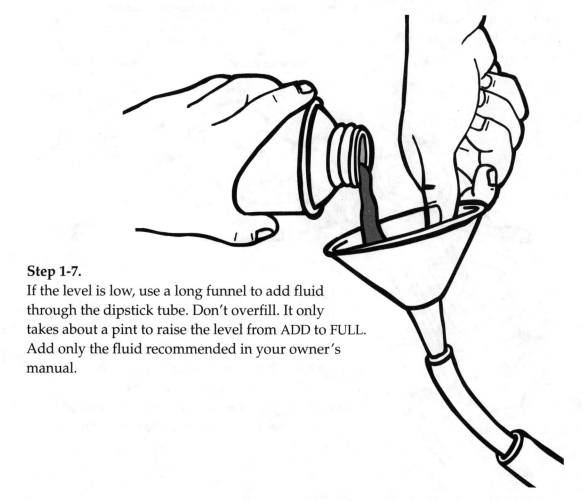

Step 1-7.
If the level is low, use a long funnel to add fluid through the dipstick tube. Don't overfill. It only takes about a pint to raise the level from ADD to FULL. Add only the fluid recommended in your owner's manual.

Step 1-8.
Locating the master cylinder.

About once a month or so, check the fluid level in the brake's master cylinder. If you have to add fluid often, check for a leak somewhere. Add only the type of brake fluid recommended for the kind of car you have. Locate the master cylinder in the engine compartment. Most import cars have see-through plastic master cylinders with maximum and minimum marks. This type of master cylinder usually has a screw cap.

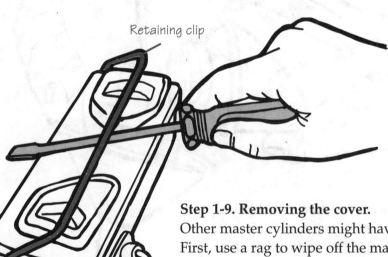

Retaining clip

Step 1-9. Removing the cover.

Other master cylinders might have a retaining clip. First, use a rag to wipe off the master cylinder cover to remove any dirt that could fall into the reservoir. Pry off the clip with a screwdriver and lift off the cover. If the reservoir is marked, the fluid level should be kept at the mark; otherwise, the fluid level should be about 1/4 inch from the top of the reservoir.

Brake fluid

Step 1-10. Adding brake fluid.

When adding brake fluid, make sure it meets the car manufacturer's recommendations. Wash off any spills with water. Brake fluid is corrosive and can damage paint. Reinstall the cover and retaining clip.

Step 1-11.
Checking the power steering fluid.

Locate the fluid reservoir next to the power steering pump. Unscrew the cap and lift it out. You should see the attached dipstick. Check the fluid level on the dipstick. The level should be between the FULL and ADD marks.

Power steering pump

Step 1-12. Removing an air filter.

The air filter is usually located in a large metal housing on top of the carburetor. Some are factory-sealed and should be checked by a professional. If your air filter is accessible, remove the cover by unscrewing the wing nut or loosening the retaining clips. Then lift out the filter.

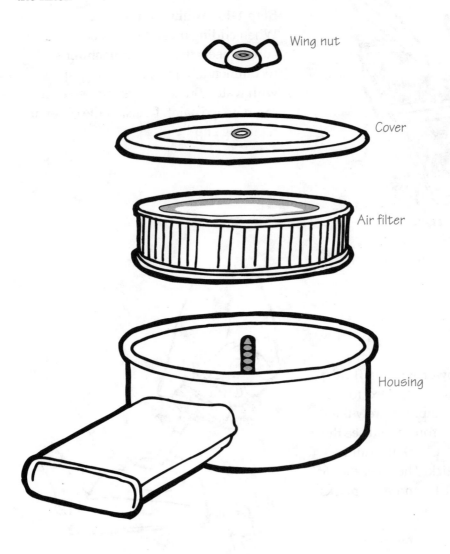

Wing nut

Cover

Air filter

Housing

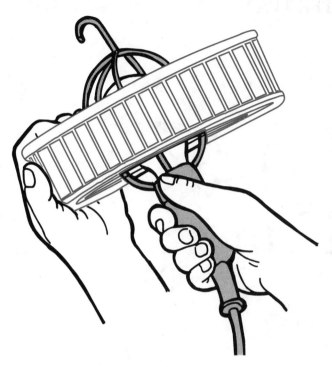

Step 1-13. Checking the filter.
Hold a light inside the filter and rotate the filter as you examine it. Look for dirt, tears, or breaks in the filter paper. If the filter is damaged or you can't see any light shining through the paper, install a new filter.

Step 1-14. Cleaning the filter.
If the filter is not damaged and light does come through the paper, it probably does not need to be replaced. Bump the bottom of the filter sharply against something to jar loose any dirt. Be careful not to dent the filter frame. If an air compressor is handy, use low pressure to blow away any dust from the inside out. Then reinstall the filter.

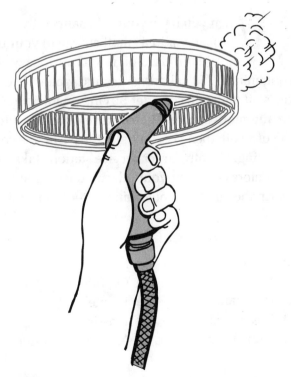

CHAPTER TWO

Changing the Oil & Oil Filter

When you have your oil changed by professionals, they probably add a small charge to your bill to cover disposal of the old oil. Used oil is a hazardous waste. One pint of oil can contaminate 750 gallons of ground water. If you decide to change your car's oil yourself, consider buying an inexpensive oil-change kit from an automotive store. These kits have basins into which you can drain the used oil; then you can take the basin to a collection center for recycling. Usually larger service stations take used oil.

Before changing your oil, run the engine a couple of minutes to warm the oil. Warm oil drains faster than cold oil.

Tools & Materials

- ❏ Wheel blocks
- ❏ Jack
- ❏ Jack stands
- ❏ Clean rags
- ❏ Drain basin
- ❏ Socket wrench
- ❏ Oil filter (strap) wrench
- ❏ Funnel
- ❏ Plastic bag
- ❏ New oil and filter

Step 2-1. Raising the car.

Set the parking brake and block the rear wheels. Use a hydraulic floor jack, if possible. Refer to the owner's manual to locate the jack points for your car. Raise the car only enough to allow room to work; then support the weight on jack stands. Never crawl under a car that is supported only by a jack.

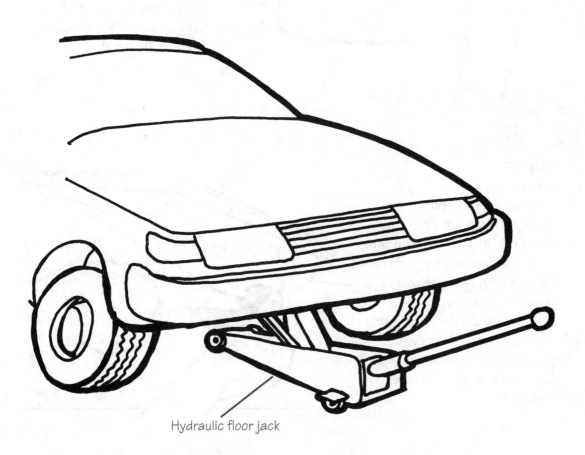

Hydraulic floor jack

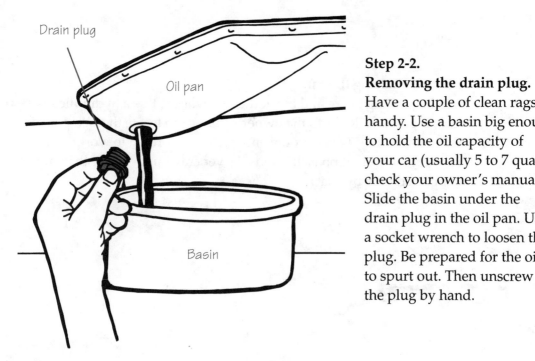

Drain plug

Oil pan

Basin

Step 2-2.
Removing the drain plug.
Have a couple of clean rags
handy. Use a basin big enough
to hold the oil capacity of
your car (usually 5 to 7 quarts;
check your owner's manual).
Slide the basin under the
drain plug in the oil pan. Use
a socket wrench to loosen the
plug. Be prepared for the oil
to spurt out. Then unscrew
the plug by hand.

Step 2-3.
Draining the oil.
Let the oil drain completely.
Wipe off the drain plug with a
clean rag. Install the drain plug
by hand; then tighten it about a
quarter turn with the socket
wrench. Some cars have
washers on the drain plug that
must be replaced every time
you change the oil. If your car
has such a washer, be sure to
replace it.

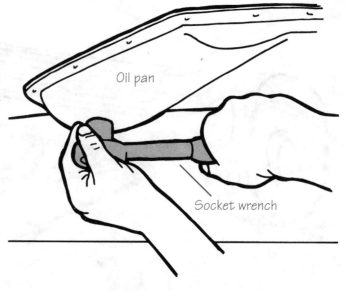

Oil pan

Socket wrench

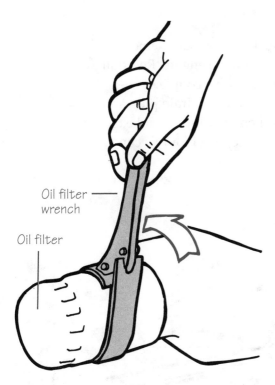

Oil filter — wrench

Oil filter

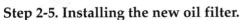

Step 2-4. Removing the oil filter.
Carefully slide the basin under the oil filter. Use an oil filter (or strap) wrench to turn the filter counterclockwise. Unscrew the filter by hand. Place the filter and the old gasket in a plastic bag. Slide the basin from beneath the car.

Step 2-5. Installing the new oil filter.
Use a clean rag to wipe the mounting stud and the mounting surface of the engine. Some filters come with gaskets installed. If yours doesn't, insert the new gasket in the groove on the filter. Now apply a thin film of new oil to the gasket and screw the new filter clockwise onto the mounting stud. Tighten the filter by hand. Most filters are now secure, but you might want to tighten it a little with the strap wrench.

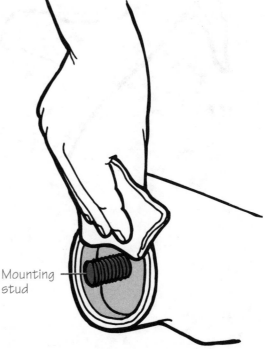

Mounting — stud

Step 2-6. Filling with oil.

Refer to the owner's manual for the oil capacity of your car. Remove the oil filler cap. Use a funnel to pour new oil into the engine. Reinstall the filler cap and start the engine. Let the engine run a couple of minutes; then turn it off. Look for any leaks around the drain plug and oil filter. Lower the car and check the oil level on the dipstick. Take the used oil and old filter to a service station that accepts oil for recycling.

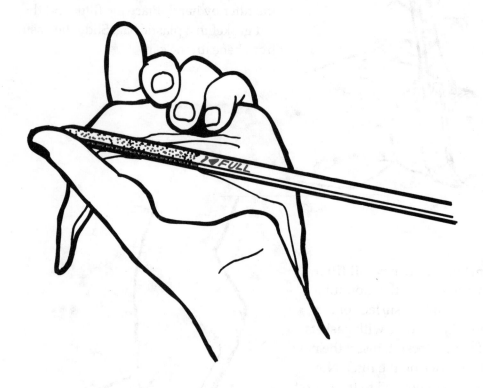

CHAPTER THREE

Car Won't Start

When you turn the key and nothing happens, or all you hear is a click, the battery might be dead, or the car might have a faulty neutral or park switch. Try wiggling the shift handle in park or neutral while turning the key. If it doesn't start, turn on the headlights and turn the key. If the headlights (or dash lights) dim or go out, the battery is weak, the battery cables are loose, or the battery terminals are corroded. Other possible causes are wet plug wires or distributor, a flooded engine, or a faulty fuel pump.

Tools & Materials

- Clean rag or paper towels
- Float battery hydrometer
- Socket wrench
- Open-ended wrench
- Screwdriver
- Pliers
- Terminal puller
- Knife
- Wire battery brush
- Baking soda
- Water
- Toothpicks
- Petroleum jelly
- Jumper cables
- Droplight

TROUBLESHOOTING GUIDE

Problem	Probable causes	Solutions
Engine won't start	Battery dead	Check battery
No sound or just a click when turning key	Loose or dirty battery cables	Clean battery post and terminals; jump start battery
	Faulty neutral or park switch in automatic transmission	Wiggle shifter in park or neutral while turning the key
Engine cranks but will not start	Battery weak	Check battery and battery terminals; charge or replace battery
	Faulty ignition system	Check spark plugs
	Faulty fuel system	Check fuel filter and fuel pump; check carburetor

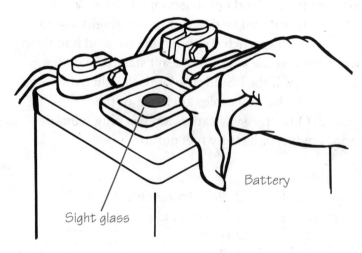

Sight glass

Battery

Step 3-1.
Checking a sealed, maintenance-free battery.
If your car has a maintenance-free battery, you should see a small window in one of the vent caps. This sight glass indicates the condition of the battery. Wipe off the glass with a paper towel or small rag.

Step 3-2.
Reading the sight glass.

If the glass is dark with a green dot, the battery is okay. If the glass is just dark, the battery might need charging. If the glass is clear, or has a yellow dot, the battery needs to be replaced.

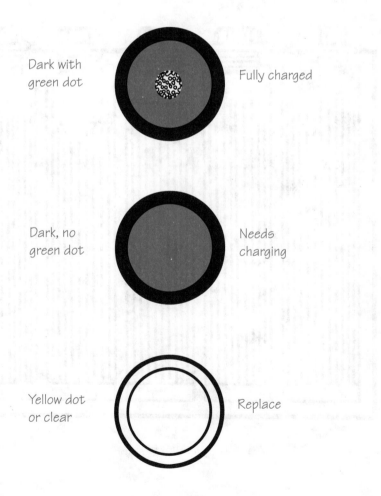

Dark with green dot — Fully charged

Dark, no green dot — Needs charging

Yellow dot or clear — Replace

Step 3-3. Checking a nonsealed battery.

A nonsealed battery has removable caps above the cells of the battery. This type of battery can be checked with a float hydrometer (Step 3-4). Remove the caps from the top of the battery and check the level of the water (electrolyte) in each cell. It should be about 1/4 inch above the top of the plates. If it isn't, add a little distilled water.

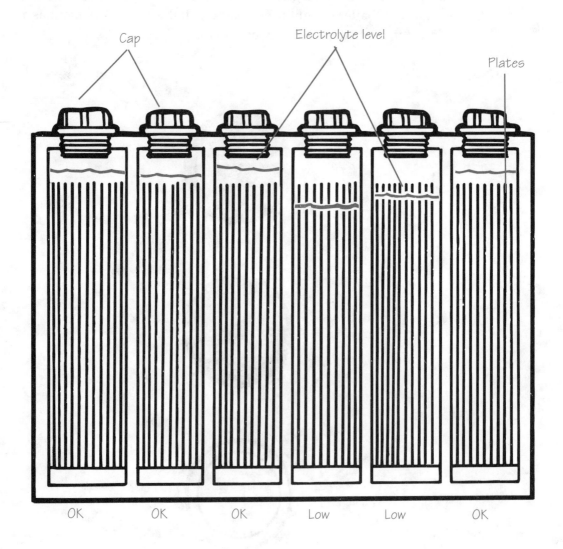

Cap   Electrolyte level   Plates

OK   OK   OK   Low   Low   OK

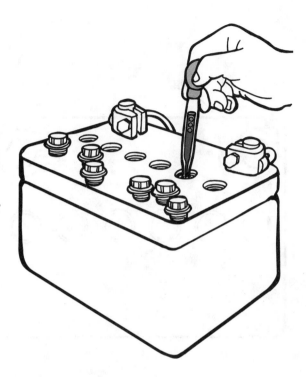

Step 3-4. Filling the hydrometer.
Insert the tip of the hydrometer into
the battery and draw up enough water
to float the balls or the float.

Step 3-5. Reading the hydrometer.
Hold the hydrometer up to eye level and compare
the number of balls floating to the chart on the
hydrometer. It might read something like "3 balls
floating, 75-percent charge." The float hydrometer has
a scale marked off on the float. Read the number at the
water line on the float. A reading of 1230 indicates
about a 75-percent charge. Release the water from the
hydrometer back into the battery and retest for
accuracy. Test each cell. If any one cell tests bad, the
battery should be replaced. If the battery is good but
the posts and clamps are corroded, you need to clean
them to allow a good connection.

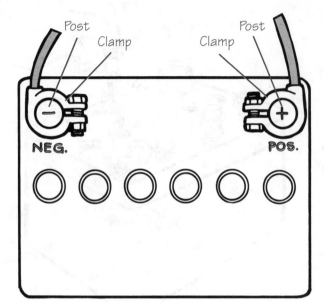

Step 3-6.
Disconnecting the battery.
Caution: The electrolyte in the battery produces highly explosive hydrogen gas. To avoid accidental sparks, always disconnect the negative cable first, and always connect the positive cable first. Never pound on a battery post when removing or connecting cable clamps.

Step 3-7.
Removing the clamps.
Use a socket wrench and an open-end wrench (1/2 or 9/16 inch), not pliers, to loosen the nut on the cable clamp. Hold the bolt with the open-ended wrench and loosen the nut with the socket wrench. On batteries with side terminals, use a box wrench to remove the terminal bolt. You can use the flat blade of a screwdriver to pry the clamps apart, but use a terminal puller for stubborn clamps.

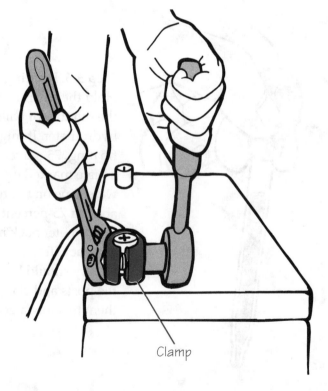

Clamp

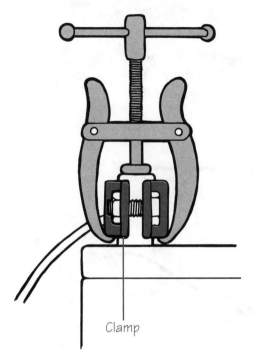

Step 3-8. Using the terminal puller.
Fit the ends of the terminal puller under the clamp and tighten the puller screw against the battery post until the clamp is free.

Clamp

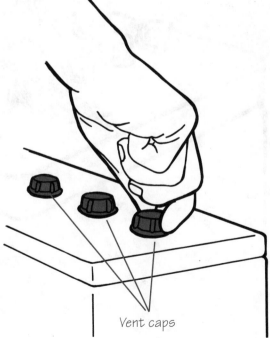

Step 3-9. Cleaning the battery.
If the battery is the nonsealed type, make sure the vent caps are tight, then temporarily plug the vent holes with toothpicks or seal them with plastic tape so that the cleaning solution does not leak into the battery.

Vent caps

Step 3-10. Neutralizing acid buildup.

Mix one heaping tablespoon of baking soda into a cup of water. This solution neutralizes the acid. Dip a soft-bristle brush into the solution, and use it to clean the top and sides of the battery. Next, rinse off the battery with clean water and dry it with paper towels. Remove the toothpicks or tape.

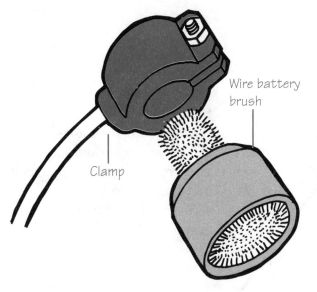

Step 3-11. Cleaning the clamps.
You can scrape the posts and the inside of the clamps with a knife or an emery board, but the best way is to use a wire battery brush. One end is designed for the posts, the other end for the clamps. Use the pointed end to clean the inside of each clamp until it shines.

Step 3-12. Cleaning the posts.
Fit the other end of the wire brush over a post. Using a twisting motion, polish each post until it shines.

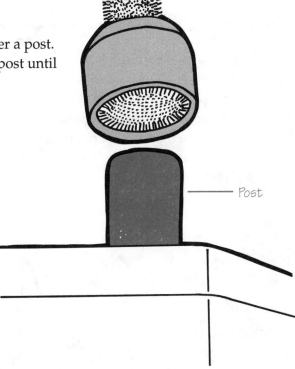

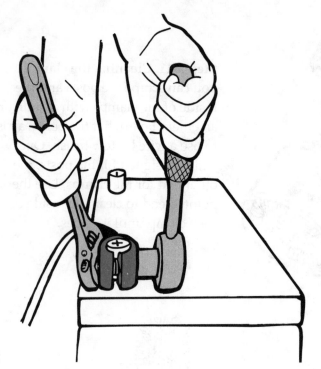

Step 3-13.
Reconnecting the cables.
Using the wrench and socket wrench, install the positive cable first and tighten the clamp securely. Then reconnect the negative cable.

Step 3-14.
Protecting the connections.
Smear a light film of petroleum jelly over each post and clamp to reduce corrosion.

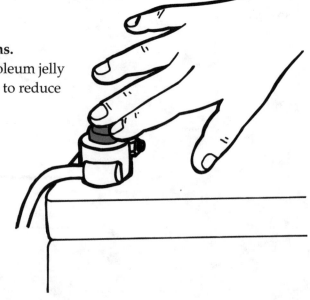

Step 3-15.
Jump-starting
a dead battery.
Make sure the batteries of
both cars have the same
voltage and that the same
terminal is grounded. Almost
all cars have the negative
terminal grounded (connected
to the engine and frame).
Move the starting car close to,
but not touching, the disabled
car. Turn off both ignitions
and all accessories. Put both
cars in PARK or NEUTRAL,
and set both hand brakes.

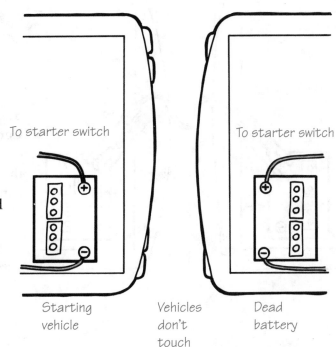

To starter switch

To starter switch

Starting
vehicle

Vehicles
don't
touch

Dead
battery

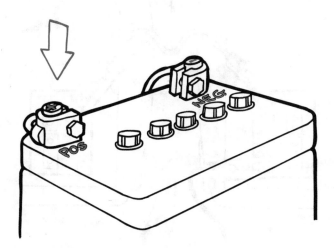

Step 3-16.
Identifying the positive post.
Locate the positive post on each
battery. It should be marked POS
and be slightly larger than the
negative post.

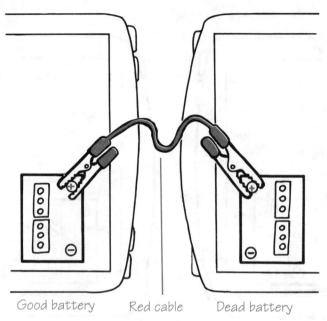

Good battery   Red cable   Dead battery

Step 3-17.
Connecting the red cable.
Connect the red jumper cable to the positive posts of both batteries.

Step 3-18.
Connecting the black cable.
Connect one end of the black jumper cable to the negative (marked NEG) post of the good battery. You should now have both ends of the red jumper cable connected to the positive posts of both batteries and one end of the black cable connected to the negative post of the good battery.

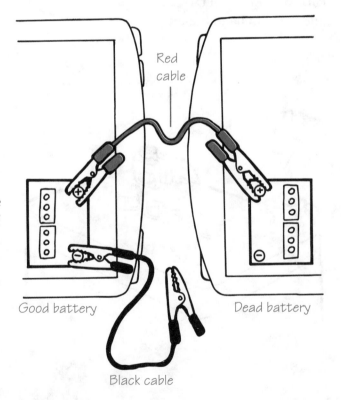

Red cable

Good battery   Dead battery

Black cable

Step 3-19.
Connecting the ground.
Connect the remaining end of the black jumper cable to a bolt on the engine or the frame of the disabled car (not the dead battery). Connect the cable at least a foot away from the dead battery, but do not connect it to the alternator or any other electrical equipment.

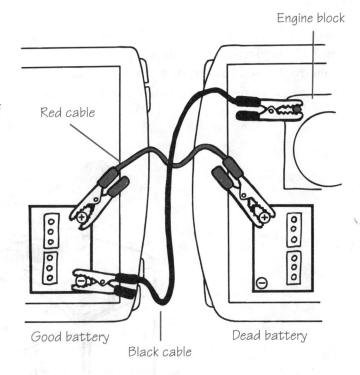

Engine block

Red cable

Good battery

Black cable

Dead battery

Step 3-20.
Starting the car.
Start the engine of the working car and bring it to a fast idle. Try to start the disabled car. Crank the engine for no more than about 10 seconds at a time, then let it cool for about 20 seconds. If it fails to start in three or four tries, something else is wrong. If it starts, disconnect the cables in the reverse order that you connected them, beginning with the black cable clamped to the bolt or frame.

Step 3-21. Replacing the battery.
To remove the old battery, first disconnect the battery
cables (negative first, then positive), and bend them
out of the way.

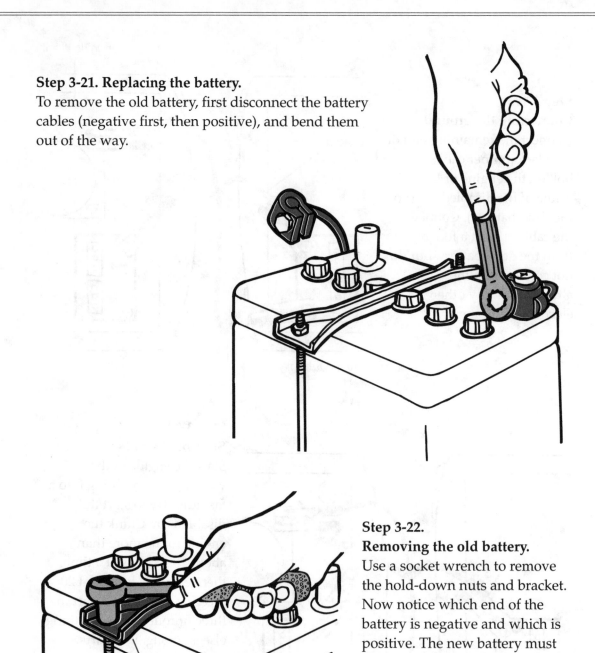

Step 3-22.
Removing the old battery.
Use a socket wrench to remove
the hold-down nuts and bracket.
Now notice which end of the
battery is negative and which is
positive. The new battery must
go in the same way. Lift the
battery from its tray.

Bracket

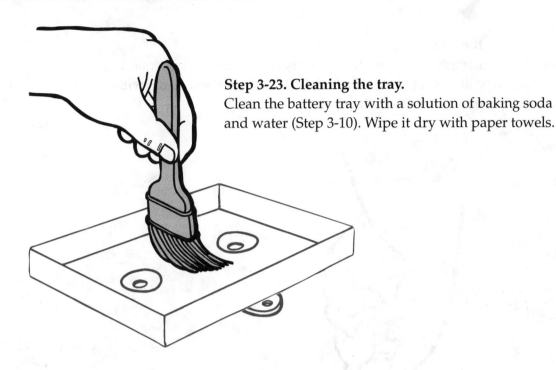

Step 3-23. Cleaning the tray.
Clean the battery tray with a solution of baking soda and water (Step 3-10). Wipe it dry with paper towels.

Step 3-24. Installing the new battery.
Carefully lower the new battery onto the clean tray. Reinstall the hold-down bracket. Tighten the hold-down nuts until they are just snug. Overtightening the nuts can crack the battery.

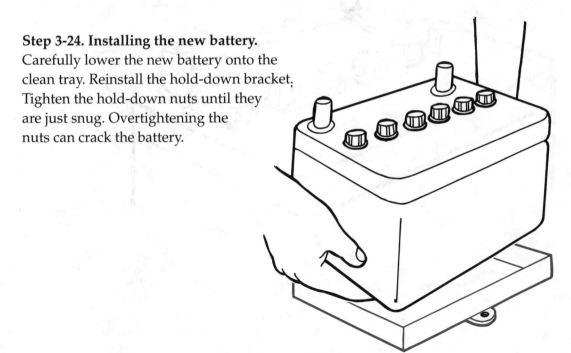

Step 3-25.
Connecting the clamps.
Polish the posts and clamps with the wire battery brush and reconnect the cables (positive first, then negative). Coat each post and clamp with a light layer of petroleum jelly.

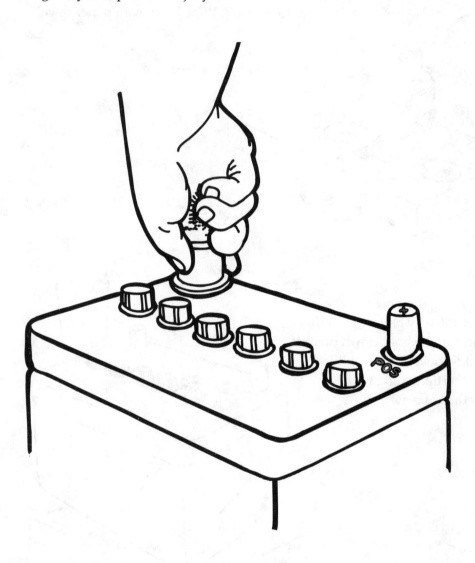

If the engine cranks but won't start, make sure all of the plug wires are connected and you see no sign of moisture. Then check the distributor.

Step 3-26. Removing the distributor cap.
Use a screwdriver to remove the distributor cap. Leave the plug wires connected to the cap. Some caps are held by two spring clips. Just pry open the clips and remove the cap. Other caps are fastened with two spring-loaded L-hooks. Press down on the hooks and turn them a quarter turn in either direction. Remove the cap.

Spring clip

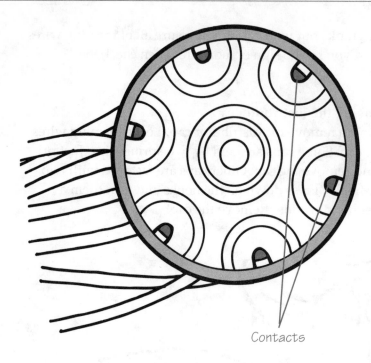

Contacts

Step 3-27.
Checking inside
the distributor cap.
Examine the inside of the
cap for any signs of pitting
or burning on the contacts.
Moisture inside the cap
guarantees problems.
Carefully wipe the inside
and outside with a clean,
dry cloth. Use a strong light
to check for any cracks in
the Bakelite surface.

Step 3-28.
Checking the cap's towers.
Remove and reinstall one
plug wire at a time by
twisting and pulling on the
boots. Check for breaks or
cracks in the cap's towers. If
the cap is good, make sure it
is clean and dry, then reinstall
it. If it has any damage at all,
install a new cap and rotor.

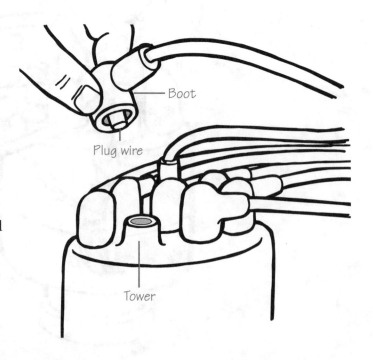

Boot

Plug wire

Tower

Step 3-29. Checking the rotor.
Some rotors are held in place with two screws. Remove the screws and lift out the rotor. Others simply lift off. Check the rotor for pitting, burning, or cracks. If it is damaged, install a new rotor and distributor cap.

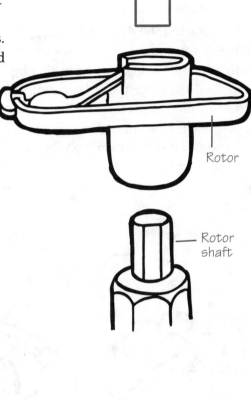

Rotor

Rotor shaft

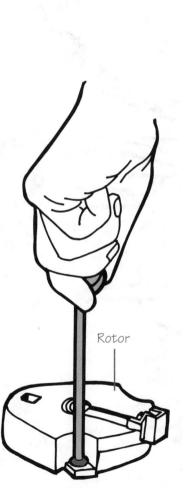

Rotor

Step 3-30. Replacing the rotor.
Fit the new rotor onto the shaft so that it is aligned. Then gently press the rotor down into position. If the rotor has screws, align the rotor with the shaft and install the screws.

Step 3-31. Replacing the distributor cap.

Install the new cap by placing it on the distributor, then gently turning the cap slightly until it drops into the aligning notches. Reattach the clips or hooks. Now place the old cap, with the wires still attached to it, next to the new one. Align the old cap with the new one. Using a starting point—the first wire after a clamp, for example—remove one wire at a time and install it firmly on the same tower on the new cap.

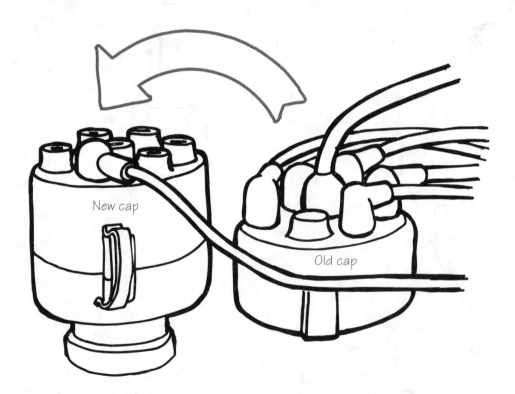

New cap

Old cap

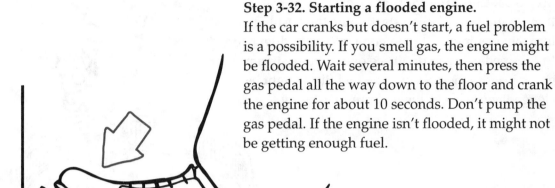

Step 3-32. Starting a flooded engine.
If the car cranks but doesn't start, a fuel problem is a possibility. If you smell gas, the engine might be flooded. Wait several minutes, then press the gas pedal all the way down to the floor and crank the engine for about 10 seconds. Don't pump the gas pedal. If the engine isn't flooded, it might not be getting enough fuel.

Gas pedal

Step 3-33. Checking the choke.
Remove the top of the air cleaner and shine a flashlight down into the carburetor. You should see the choke plate. If the engine is warm, the plate should be open. If the engine is cold, the plate should be closed. If the engine is cold and the plate isn't closed, push it closed and try to start the engine.

Air filter

Choke plate

Step 3-34. Checking for fuel.

If the engine still doesn't start, shine the flashlight down
into the opening while someone presses suddenly on
the gas pedal. If you don't see one or more streams of
gas spurt into the opening, the fuel filter might be
clogged; more likely, the fuel pump is faulty.

Air filter

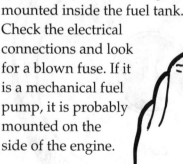

Step 3-35. Checking the fuel pump.

If no gas spurted into the carburetor and the fuel filter is not clogged
(see chapter 3), the fuel pump is probably faulty. Disconnect the fuel
line from the carburetor. Hold the end of the fuel line over a can or jar
and have someone briefly crank the engine. Make sure you direct the
fuel line into the can to catch the gas. And only briefly crank the
engine. You should see steady, consistent spurts of gas. If little or no
gas spurts from the fuel line, the fuel pump is probably bad and needs
to be replaced. If it is an electric fuel pump (some imports and cars
with fuel injection), it might be
mounted inside the fuel tank.
Check the electrical
connections and look
for a blown fuse. If it
is a mechanical fuel
pump, it is probably
mounted on the
side of the engine.

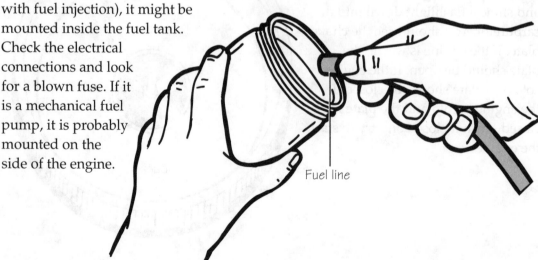

Fuel line

Step 3-36. Removing a mechanical fuel pump.
Follow the fuel line from the carburetor back to the fuel pump.
Disconnect the fuel lines from the pump and plug the line from the
tank with a wooden pencil, bolt, or something similar. The gas from the
tank gravity-feeds to the pump, so you can drain the tank if you don't
plug the line.

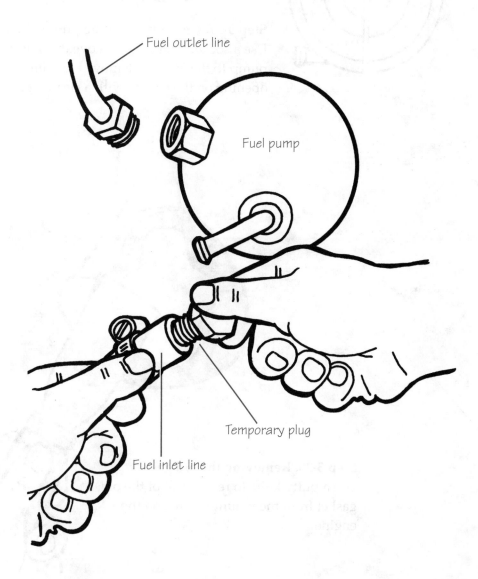

Fuel outlet line

Fuel pump

Temporary plug

Fuel inlet line

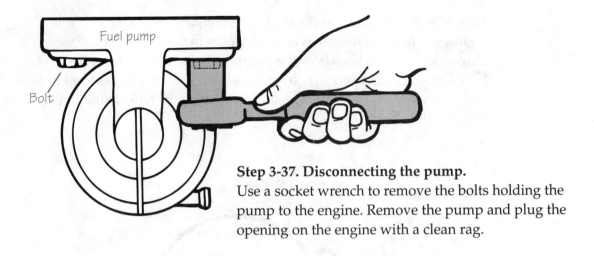

Step 3-37. Disconnecting the pump.
Use a socket wrench to remove the bolts holding the pump to the engine. Remove the pump and plug the opening on the engine with a clean rag.

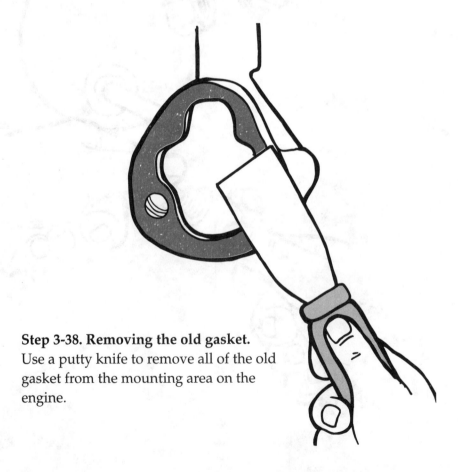

Step 3-38. Removing the old gasket.
Use a putty knife to remove all of the old gasket from the mounting area on the engine.

Step 3-39.
Installing a mechanical fuel pump.

You will notice a rocker arm on the pump. Remove the rag and use a flashlight to look inside the engine. You should see a pushrod or a lobe on the engine camshaft. Make sure the rocker arm comes into full contact with the lobe or fits under the pushrod. Apply a thin layer of gasket sealer to the mounting area on the engine and the same area on the new pump. Now fit the new gasket to the pump, making sure the holes line up.

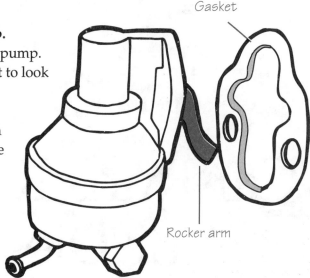

Gasket

Rocker arm

Step 3-40. Mounting the pump.

To mount the pump, insert the rocker arm at a slight downward angle, then push in on the pump until it is in full contact with the engine. Install the mounting bolts by hand, then tighten with the socket wrench. Remove the temporary plug and reconnect the fuel lines. Start the car and check for any leaks.

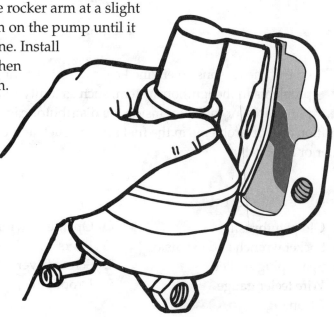

CHAPTER FOUR

Car Runs Rough or Dies

S ome of the reasons an engine keeps dying or running rough are problems in the ignition system, such as faulty plugs, wet or bad plug wires, or moisture inside the distributor cap or around the ignition coil; or problems in the fuel system, such as a clogged fuel filter or PCV valve.

Tools & Materials

- ❏ Old paintbrush
- ❏ Socket wrench and extension
- ❏ Spark plug socket
- ❏ Wire feeler gauge
- ❏ Clean rag
- ❏ Open-end wrenches
- ❏ Pliers
- ❏ Screwdriver
- ❏ Droplight

TROUBLESHOOTING GUIDE

Problem	Probable causes	Solutions
Car runs rough or keeps dying	Faulty ignition system	Check spark plugs, plug wires, distributor cap, rotor and ignition coil
	Faulty PCV valve	Check PCV valve and hose
	Faulty fuel system	Check fuel filter, fuel pump; check carburetor

Step 4-1. Checking spark plug wires.

If the engine starts but runs rough, the problem might be faulty spark plugs. First, make sure the plug wires are firmly connected to each plug and to the distributor cap. Check each wire for breaks or burns in the insulation. If the wires look fine, check the plugs.

Plug wire

Engine block

Spark plug boot

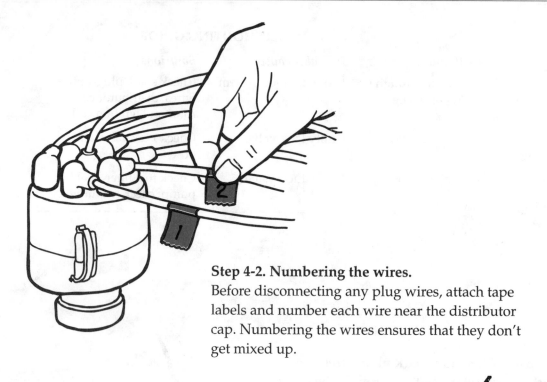

Step 4-2. Numbering the wires.
Before disconnecting any plug wires, attach tape labels and number each wire near the distributor cap. Numbering the wires ensures that they don't get mixed up.

Step 4-3. Disconnecting the wires.
The spark plugs are located on the engine block. The wires are attached with boots similar to those on the distributor cap. Don't pull on the wire—gently twist the boot and pull it from the plug. Use an old paintbrush to brush away any dirt from around the plug so that none can fall into the hole when the plug is removed.

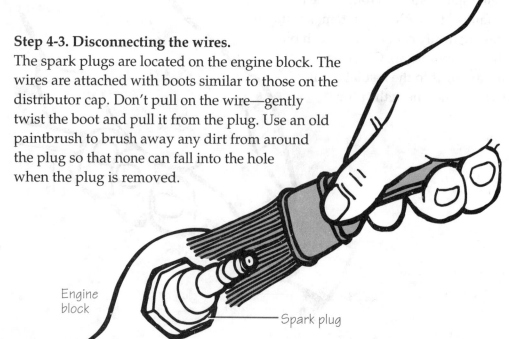

Engine
block

Spark plug

Step 4-4. Removing the plugs.
Use a spark plug socket (it might be 13/16 or 5/8 inch, or 14 or 18 mm, depending on the car). Push the socket over the plug, making sure that the rubber insert inside the socket fits snugly. Now use a socket wrench and extension (a universal joint might be necessary) to loosen the plug. Turn the wrench counterclockwise to free the plug; then remove the plug by hand.

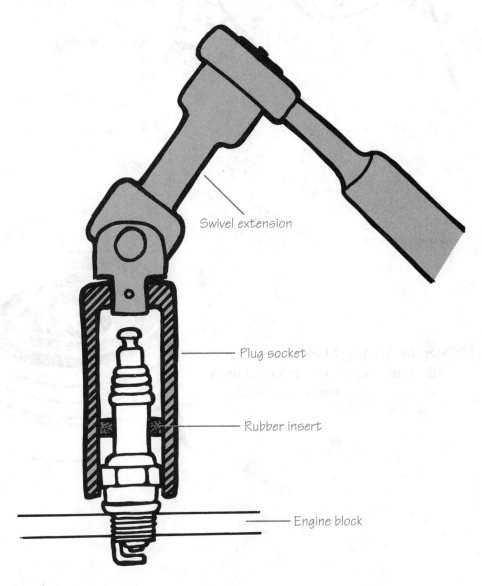

Swivel extension

Plug socket

Rubber insert

Engine block

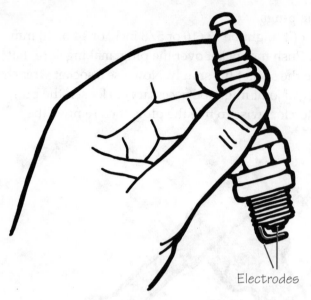

Electrodes

Step 4-5. Checking the plugs.
Examine the plug for cracks or burns in the porcelain. Check to see if the electrodes are burned. The area around the electrodes should be colored tan.

Step 4-6. Finding black plugs.
If the plug is black, it hasn't been firing. The plug or plug wire might be bad.

Step 4-7.
Finding carbon on the plugs.
If the area around the electrodes is covered with black, sooty carbon deposits, the cause might be slow, stop-and-go driving or too rich a fuel mixture due to a sticking choke or clogged air cleaner.

Step 4-8. Finding oily plugs.
If the plug has a wet, oily coating, oil might be leaking past the rings or valve guides. Or the problem might be something as simple as a plugged PCV valve. When in doubt, install new plugs.

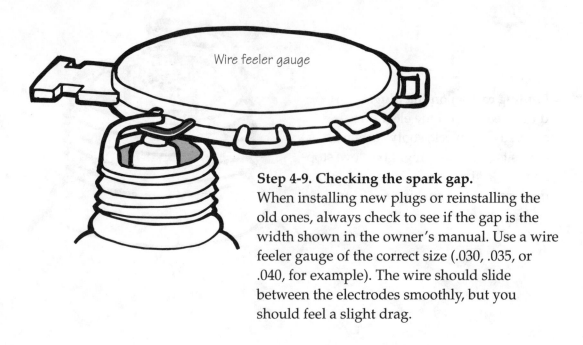

Step 4-9. Checking the spark gap.

When installing new plugs or reinstalling the old ones, always check to see if the gap is the width shown in the owner's manual. Use a wire feeler gauge of the correct size (.030, .035, or .040, for example). The wire should slide between the electrodes smoothly, but you should feel a slight drag.

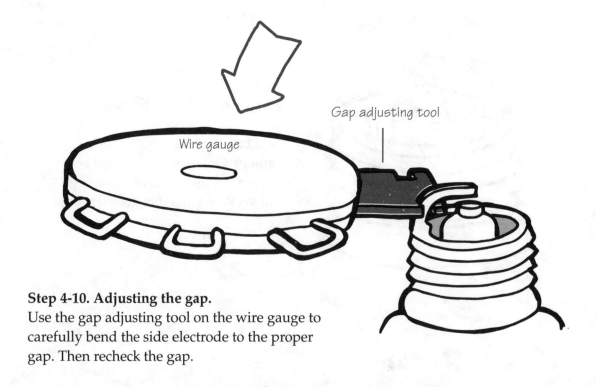

Step 4-10. Adjusting the gap.

Use the gap adjusting tool on the wire gauge to carefully bend the side electrode to the proper gap. Then recheck the gap.

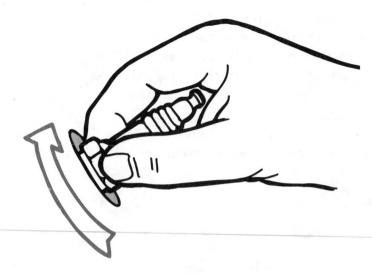

Step 4-11.
Installing spark plugs.
Thread the plug into the hole by hand, being careful not to cross-thread it. Turn the plug clockwise until it is firmly seated in the hole.

Step 4-12. Tightening the plugs.
Slide the spark plug socket over the plug, fit the socket wrench and extension into the socket and tighten the plug one-quarter turn if the plug has a gasket. If the plug has a tapered seat (no gasket), tighten it one-sixteenth of a turn after it has been seated. Reconnect the plug wires by pressing the boot firmly over the spark plug. Be sure to route the wires as they were before you disconnected them.

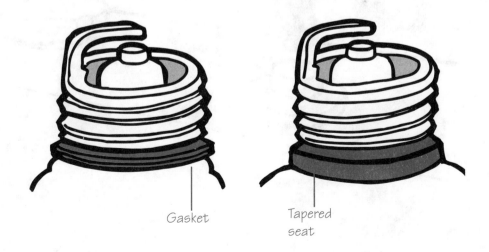

Gasket

Tapered
seat

Step 4-13. Checking and replacing the PCV valve.

The PCV valve is a vacuum-operated valve. It controls the amount of escaped gases from the crankcase that are recycled back into the combustion chamber, where they are reburned. It is usually plugged into the valve cover or the oil filler cap and is attached to a hose. The hose runs to the air cleaner or intake manifold. Simply unplug the PCV valve and shake it. If you don't hear it rattle, it is bad and needs to be replaced. Pull and twist the old valve from the hose and install a new one. Plug the new valve back in the engine.

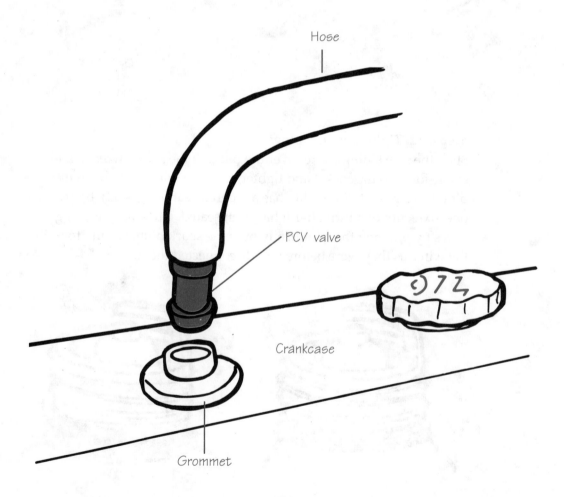

Hose

PCV valve

Crankcase

Grommet

A classic example of a clogged fuel filter occurs when the
acts like its running out of gas, usually at highway speeds. Th
starts normally, runs a mile or so, and then dies again.

Step 4-14. Removing the fuel filter on a General Motors car.
First remove the air cleaner assembly. The fuel filter is located inside
the carburetor behind a large fuel inlet nut. Place a rag below the nut to
catch any spilled gas. Hold the larger inlet nut with one wrench. Turn
the smaller nut on the fuel line counterclockwise with another wrench
to disconnect the fuel line. Remove the larger nut and gasket. A spring
behind the filter will push the filter out.

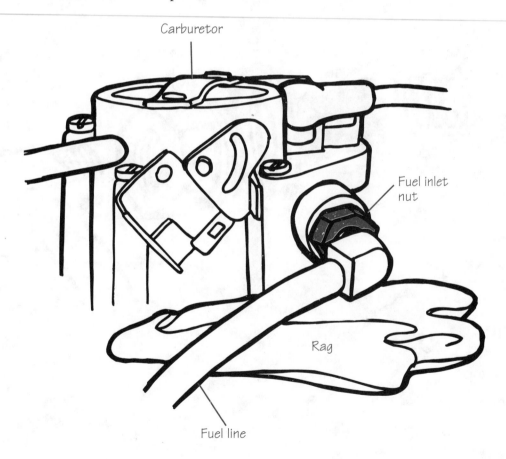

Carburetor

Fuel inlet
nut

Rag

Fuel line

Step 4-15. Installing the new fuel filter on a GM car.

Install the new filter and new gasket and thread the larger nut on by hand, then tighten it with the wrench. Now reconnect the fuel line by hand. Hold the larger nut with one wrench and tighten the smaller nut with the other wrench. Remove the rag and start the engine to check for leaks. If the fitting leaks, turn off the engine and tighten the connections.

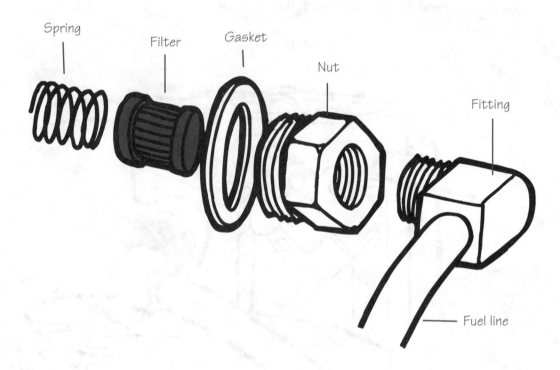

Spring   Filter   Gasket   Nut   Fitting   Fuel line

Step 4-16. Removing the fuel filter on a Ford car.
First remove the air cleaner. A Ford fuel filter is screwed into the
carburetor. The fuel line is connected to the filter by a hose fastened
with clamps. Place a rag below the filter to catch any spilled gas. Use
pliers or a screwdriver to loosen the hose clamp. Slide the clamps off
the hose. Now twist and pull the hose from the end of the filter.
Unscrew the filter counterclockwise with a wrench.

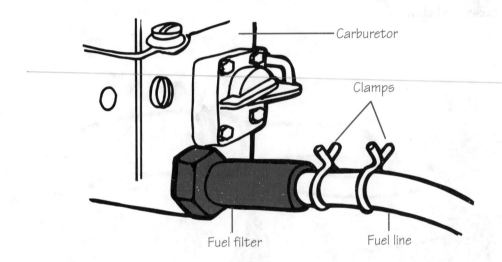

Carburetor

Clamps

Fuel filter   Fuel line

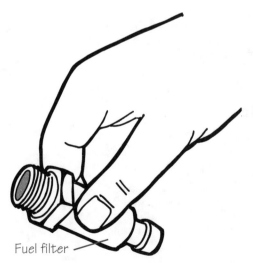

Fuel filter

Step 4-17.
Installing the new fuel filter on a Ford.
Thread the new filter in place by hand. Then
tighten with a wrench. *Caution:* This type of
filter might have a tapered thread, so the nut
part of the filter might not fit flush against
the carburetor. If the hose was damaged,
replace it. If not, reconnect it to the new
filter, remove the rag, and start the engine to
check for leaks.

Step 4-18.
Locating the fuel filter on an AMC, Chrysler, or import car.
On these cars, the filter is located in the fuel line somewhere between the fuel pump and the carburetor. It might be mounted in a bracket under the hood, or, on some imports, inside a rear fender well near the gas tank. Trace the fuel line to locate the filter. It is a disposable canister made of see-through plastic that allows you to see the amount of dirt trapped in the filter. The filter is connected to the metal fuel line by hoses and clamps.

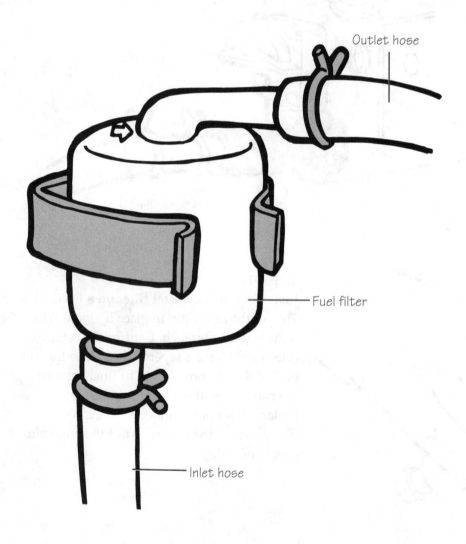

Outlet hose

Fuel filter

Inlet hose

Step 4-19.
Removing the filter
from an AMC, Chrysler, or import.
Place a rag underneath the filter to catch any spilled gas. Release any retaining clip holding the filter in the bracket. Use a screwdriver or pliers to remove the clamp from the hoses. Twist the hoses from the filter and remove the filter. Examine the old filter. You will see an inlet and outlet marked on the filter with an arrow. Be sure to install the new filter according to the direction of the fuel flow indicated by the arrow.

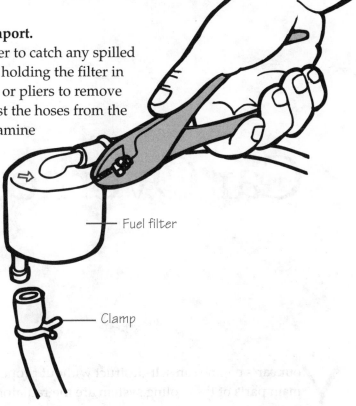

Fuel filter

Clamp

Step 4-20.
Installing the new filter
on an AMC, Chrysler, or import.
Examine the new filter and note the direction of the arrow. Install the new filter in the direction of the arrow. If the hoses are damaged, install new hoses. Reconnect the hoses and tighten the clamps. Place the filter back in the bracket and fasten any retaining clip. Remove the rag, start the car, and check for leaks.

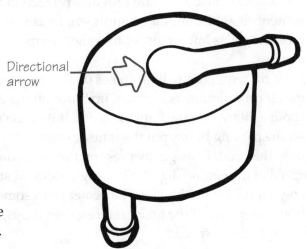

Directional arrow

CHAPTER FIVE

Car Overheats

Your car's engine can self-destruct without proper cooling. The main parts of the cooling system are the radiator, pressure cap, thermostat, water pump, hoses, fan, and fan belt. The system should be filled year-round with a 50/50 or 60/40 mixture of antifreeze and water. A 50/50 mixture provides protection to about–34 degrees Fahrenheit, while undiluted antifreeze freezes at about–8 degrees. If the coolant level is low, or any of the other components fail, the engine can overheat.

If the temperature light comes on (or the gauge starts to rise) and the air conditioning is running, first turn off the air conditioner. Allow about a minute for the light to go out. If it doesn't, find a place to park, set the parking brake, put the transmission in PARK or NEUTRAL and raise the hood. Now gently press on the gas pedal to increase the idle speed of the engine slightly. The engine should start to cool. If not, turn on your heater and blower. The heater pulls some of the heat away from the engine. If the temperature gauge drops, continue on your way, but at a slower speed.

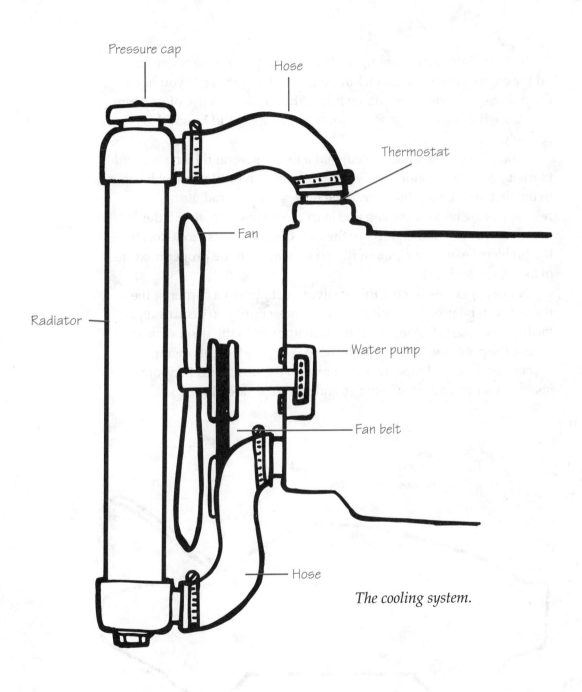

The cooling system.

If the radiator starts boiling, quickly find a place to park and turn off the engine. Raise the hood, but don't touch anything. If you open the radiator cap when the engine is hot, the sudden release of pressure will cause the coolant to boil. You or a bystander could be scalded severely.

When the radiator has cooled, fold a rag to several thicknesses and place it over the radiator cap. Slowly turn the cap until you feel it come to the first notch. Stop there until the pressure in the radiator is released. Now remove the cap and start the engine. Slowly fill the radiator with water, then replace the cap. Check the system to locate the problem. After the repair, refill the system with the proper mixture of antifreeze and water.

For emergencies, keep a roll of silver duct tape in a corner of the trunk. It can be used to patch a ruptured hose until you get to a repair facility. If a hose is leaking, turn the radiator cap to the first notch to relieve the pressure. Make sure the hose is dry, then tightly wrap several turns of duct tape over the break in the hose. This temporary fix just might keep you from being stranded on the side of the road.

Raise the hood carefully to avoid getting burned by the steam.

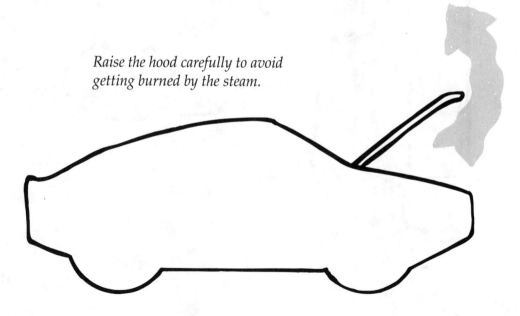

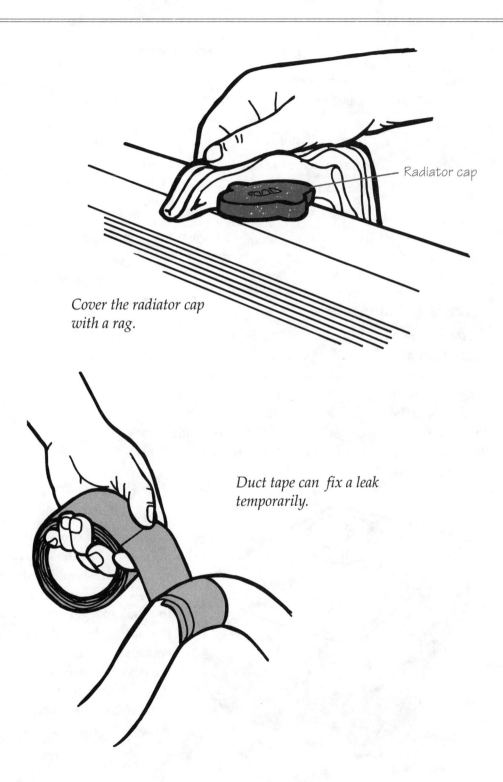

Radiator cap

Cover the radiator cap
with a rag.

Duct tape can fix a leak
temporarily.

TROUBLESHOOTING GUIDE

Problem	Probable causes	Solutions
Car overheats	Coolant level low	Add coolant; check hoses and hose clamps
	Clogged radiator	Check radiator for debris
	Broken or loose fan belt	Check fan belt
	Faulty radiator cap	Check radiator cap
	Faulty thermostat	Check thermostat
	Faulty water pump	Have water pump checked

Tools & Materials

- ❏ Large rag
- ❏ Clean pan
- ❏ Wrench
- ❏ Clean water
- ❏ Garden hose
- ❏ Coolant hydrometer
- ❏ Needle-nose pliers
- ❏ Screwdriver
- ❏ Socket wrench
- ❏ Pliers
- ❏ Sharp knife
- ❏ Emery cloth
- ❏ Wire brush
- ❏ Rubber mallet
- ❏ Putty knife

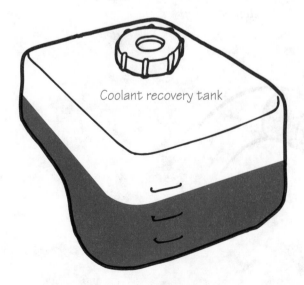

Coolant recovery tank

Step 5-1.
Checking the coolant level.
If the car has a coolant recovery system, you should find a plastic tank somewhere near the radiator. Check the coolant level using the marks on the side of the plastic tank. Add coolant to the tank, not the radiator. If the plastic tank is empty, or if the car does not have a coolant recovery system, let the radiator cool, and then remove the cap to check the level.

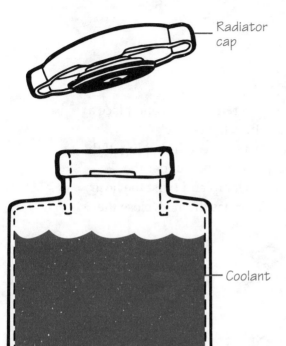

Radiator
cap

Coolant

Step 5-2. Removing the cap.
If the system is the least bit warm, cover the radiator cap with a folded cloth. Turn the cap to the first notch to release the pressure. When the hissing stops, push down on the cap with the heel of your hand and turn it the rest of the way. If the cap has a lever, lift the lever to release the pressure. Remove the cap. The coolant level should be 1 or 2 inches below the filler neck.

Step 5-3. Checking the cap.
Check the cap for a worn or cracked gasket. If it is damaged, install a new cap. The caps for radiators with recovery systems are not interchangeable. Be sure to buy the proper cap for your system. Check for rust on the cap and inside the filler neck on the radiator. Flush the system if you find any rust.

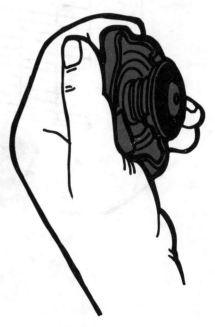

Step 5-4. Draining the radiator.

First make sure the engine is cool. Remove the radiator cap and place a clean pan under the drain petcock or plug. Turn the petcock counterclockwise to open it. Use a wrench to remove a drain plug. If the radiator does not have a petcock or plug, place the pan under the bottom radiator-hose connection. Loosen the clamp and twist the hose from the neck of the radiator. After the radiator has drained, close the petcock or reinstall the plug or bottom hose.

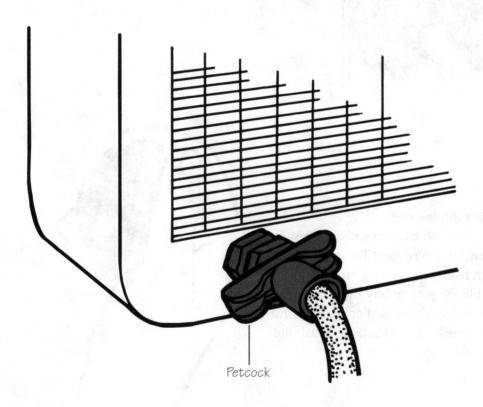

Petcock

Step 5-5. Flushing the system.

After the radiator has drained, fill it with clean water and install the pressure cap. Set the parking brake and put the transmission in NEUTRAL or PARK. Start the engine and turn the heater on high. Let the engine idle for a few minutes. Then, being careful of the fan, feel the top radiator hose. When the hose gets hot, the thermostat has opened and water is circulating through the engine. Allow the engine to idle a few more minutes, then turn it off and drain the system again. Repeat the steps (filling the radiator, running the engine, and draining) until the drained water runs clear. Four or five times should be enough. If the radiator has a coolant recovery system, flush the plastic tank with clean water and leave it empty. Close the petcock or reinstall the plug or bottom hose.

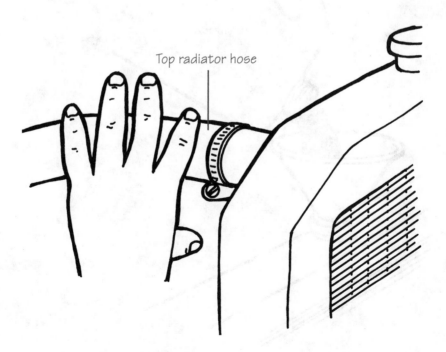

Top radiator hose

Step 5-6. Filling the radiator.

Check your owner's manual to determine the capacity of your cooling system. Depending on the car, it might hold between 5 and 13 quarts of coolant. Pour in the correct amount of antifreeze to provide a 50/50 or 60/40 mixture of antifreeze and water. Add water to bring the level within an inch or two of the filler neck. Start the engine with the radiator cap off and let the engine run for about 15 minutes. Turn off the engine and check the coolant level. If your car has a coolant recovery system, the level should be at the overflow tube and at the full mark on the plastic tank. Without the recovery system, the level should be 1 or 2 inches below the filler neck. Add antifreeze and water to bring the coolant to the proper level. Install the radiator cap.

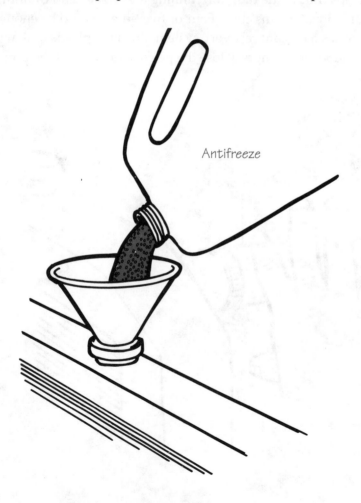

Antifreeze

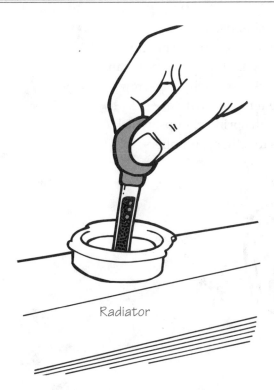

Radiator

Step 5-7. Testing the coolant.
To test the coolant, carefully remove the radiator cap and place the end of the tube on the hydrometer into the coolant. Use the bulb to draw coolant up into the hydrometer. Some hydrometers use floating balls; others might have a float with a scale. The reading on the hydrometer indicates the coldest temperature to which the coolant provides protection.

Step 5-8. Cleaning debris from the radiator.
Remove leaves and larger pieces of debris by hand. Wash away smaller pieces with a garden hose. Try to spray from the back of the radiator to the front. Carefully straighten any bent fins with needle-nose pliers. The fins are soft, so be careful not to damage them.

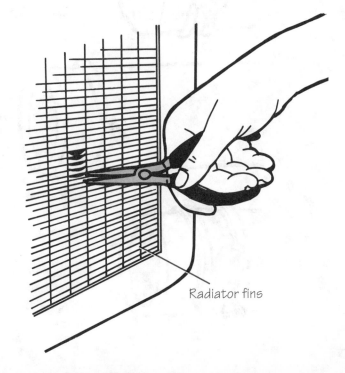

Radiator fins

Step 5-9. Removing different types of hose clamps.

You might find one of four different types of hose clamps. The most reliable and easiest to work with is the worm-gear type. This type can be loosened with a screwdriver or a small socket wrench. The screw clamp type is made of two wires and can be removed with a screwdriver. The remaining two types are both spring clamps, which can be removed by squeezing the bent ends together with pliers.

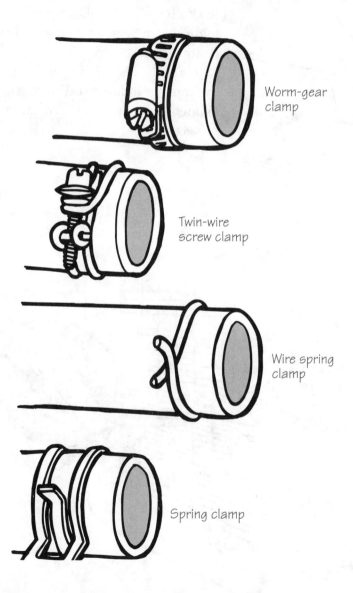

Worm-gear clamp

Twin-wire screw clamp

Wire spring clamp

Spring clamp

Step 5-10. Removing the hose clamps.

First remove the radiator cap, place a clean pan under the drain petcock, and drain the radiator down to below the level of the hose. Loosen both hose clamps and slide them toward the middle of the hose.

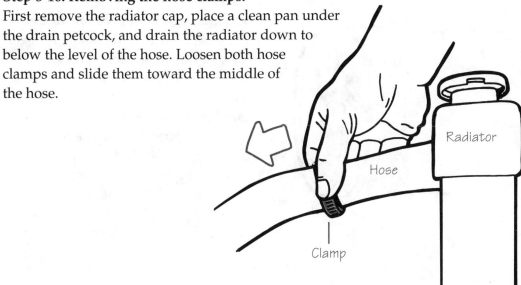

Step 5-11. Removing a stubborn hose.

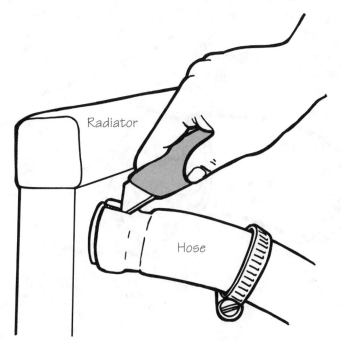

If the hose doesn't twist off after a few tries, slit both ends of the hose with a sharp knife. Do not pry the hose off with a screwdriver. The radiator neck is made of soft metal and is easily dented. Twist the hose free and discard it. Clean the neck on the radiator with a piece of emery cloth. Clean the connection on the engine with a wire brush.

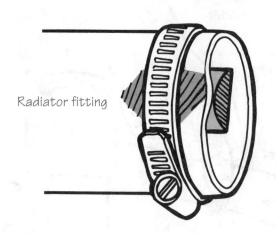

Radiator fitting

Step 5-12.
Straightening a bent radiator fitting.
If the pipe to the radiator happens to get bent, don't try to hammer it back into shape. You could loosen the soldered connections. Fit a worm-gear hose clamp around the damaged end of the pipe. Tighten the clamp to form the proper shape. Place an object that is half-round (a wooden broom handle, for example) against the bend. Then use pliers to press the bend back to the inside of the clamp, bringing the pipe back to its original shape.

Step 5-13. Installing a new radiator hose.
Some radiator hoses are made with bends and curves to fit the engine. Be sure you have the proper hose. If the hose clamps are rusty or damaged, install new ones. Slide the hose clamps over each end of the new hose. Wet the inside of the hose with a little water to help it slide onto the connections. Slide the ends of the hose onto the connections. Position the clamps so that they are about 1/4 inch from each end of the hose, and tighten the clamps.

Curved radiator hose

Step 5-14. Refilling the radiator.
Close the petcock, refill the
radiator (see Step 5-6), and start
the engine with the radiator cap
off. When the engine reaches
operating temperature, turn it off
and check the coolant level. Add
coolant if necessary and install
the radiator cap. Start the engine
and let it run three or four
minutes to build up pressure in
the coolant system. Turn off the
engine and check the hose
connections for leaks.

Drain petcock

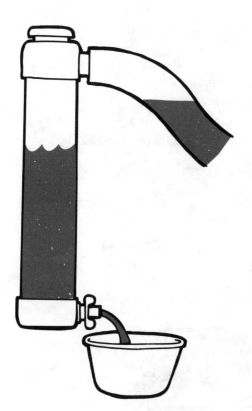

Step 5-15. Replacing the thermostat.
Place a pan beneath the radiator drain
petcock. Drain enough coolant to lower the
level down below the top radiator hose.
Save the coolant—you can reuse it if it is not
too old.

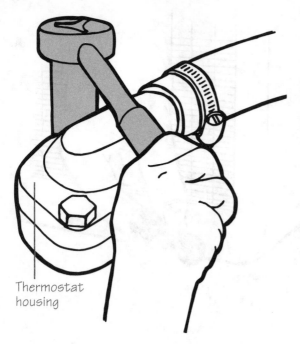

Thermostat
housing

Step 5-16. Removing the thermostat. You usually do not need to disconnect the top radiator hose. Use a socket wrench to remove the two bolts holding the thermostat housing to the engine. You might have to tap the housing lightly with a rubber mallet to break the gasket seal. Lift off the housing and remove the thermostat. Notice how the thermostat was positioned in the engine opening.

Step 5-17. Removing the old gasket.
Stuff a clean rag in the opening. Then use a putty knife, not a screwdriver, to scrape the old gasket material from the engine and thermostat housing. Be sure to clean any indentations to allow for a smooth fit. Otherwise, you might create a leak or break the ears on the housing during the reassembly.

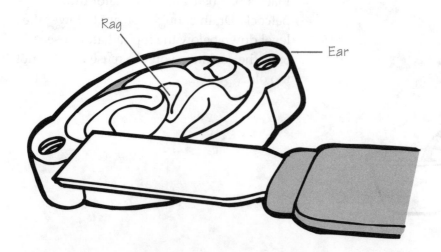

Rag

Ear

Step 5-18.
Installing the new thermostat.
Remove the rag from the engine opening. Hold the new thermostat with the spring end down and insert it in the opening. If required, apply a thin layer of nonhardening silicone gasket sealer to the cleaned surfaces around the openings. Install the new gasket on the engine opening, making sure it is aligned with the holes.

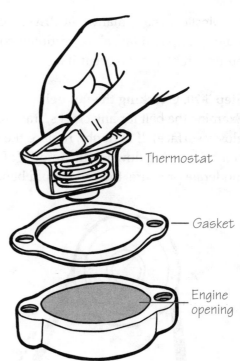

Thermostat

Gasket

Engine opening

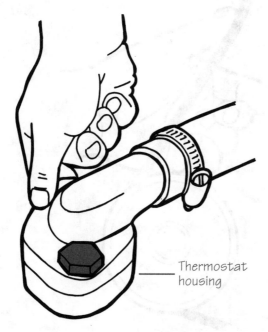

Thermostat housing

Step 5-19.
Mounting the housing.
Fit the thermostat housing over the engine opening and screw the two bolts in by hand. Use a socket wrench to tighten the bolts evenly, but don't overtighten. Refill the radiator with coolant. Set the parking brake, place the transmission in NEUTRAL or PARK, and idle the engine until it reaches operating temperature. Check for leaks.

Most cars have many belt-driven accessories such as the alternator, water pump and fan, air conditioner compressor, and power steering pump. Problems can occur if a belt is too loose, too tight, or damaged.

Step 5-20. Checking the fan belt.
Examine the belt for any cracks, fraying, or severe glazing (shiny or glossy surface). If in doubt, replace the belt. Check the tension of the belt by pressing down in the middle of the belt with your thumb. With moderate pressure, the belt should bend about 1/2 inch.

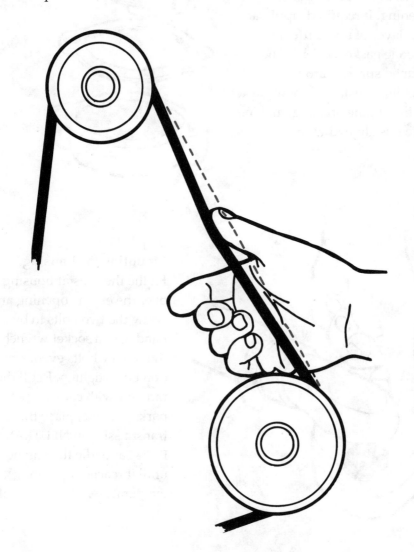

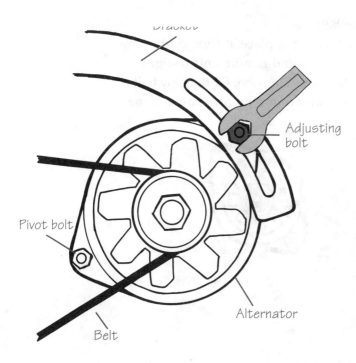

Bracket

Adjusting
bolt

Pivot bolt

Alternator

Belt

Step 5-21.
Loosening the alternator.
Use a wrench to loosen the adjusting bolt in the slotted bracket holding the alternator. You also might need to loosen the bolt that the alternator pivots on. You should now be able to move the alternator in the adjusting bracket.

Step 5-22.
Removing the old fan belt.
If the fan belt is behind other belts, the other belts must be removed first. Then push the alternator toward the engine until the belt slackens enough so that you can remove it. Remove the belt from the alternator pulley and crankshaft pulley. If you can't get enough slack in the belt, and the alternator is pushed all the way in its slotted bracket, cut the belt with a sharp knife.

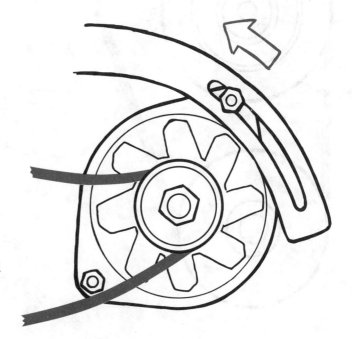

Step 5-23. Installing the new fan belt.

Be sure you have the right fan belt. When in place, it should fit even with the top of the pulley groove and should require only a slight adjustment of the alternator for the proper tension. Fit the new belt over the crankshaft pulley and the water pump pulley. Now roll the belt over the alternator pulley.

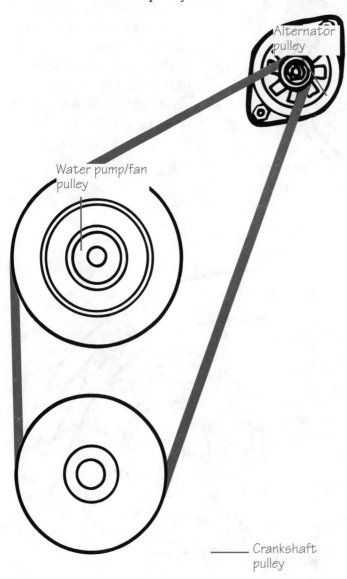

Alternator pulley

Water pump/fan pulley

Crankshaft pulley

Step 5-24. Adjusting the belt.

Pull the alternator out away from the engine by hand. If a pry bar must be used, be careful not to lean it against the alternator fins. Apply enough pressure on the alternator until the belt has the proper tension, then tighten the adjusting bolt and, if loosened, the pivot bolt. Start the engine and let it run a few minutes. Then turn off the engine and recheck the tension.

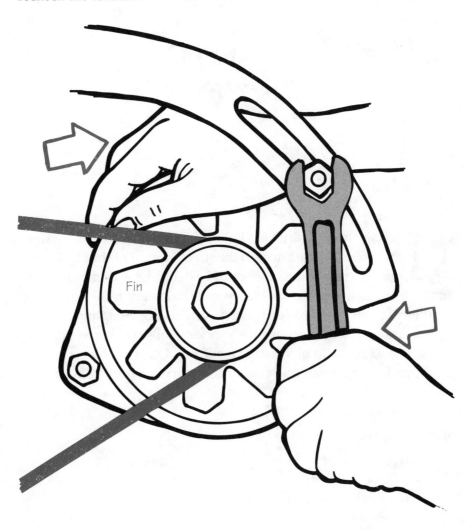

CHAPTER SIX

Lights

Most cars have a variety of lights to illuminate everything from the glove compartment to the street in front of the car. Cars manufactured since 1985 even have eye-level brake lights to alert those inattentive drivers behind you. Fortunately, troubleshooting the lighting system is not too difficult. Nearly half of all lighting problems are caused by corroded bulb sockets, loose or corroded ground connections, bad bulbs, or blown fuses. Other problems can be caused by a loose alternator belt (see chapter 5) or a faulty relay or flasher.

Tools & Materials

- ❏ Phillips screwdriver
- ❏ Masking tape
- ❏ Small flat-blade screwdriver
- ❏ Fine sandpaper
- ❏ Emery cloth
- ❏ Fuse puller

TROUBLESHOOTING GUIDE

Problem	Probable causes	Solutions
Lights flicker or won't burn	Loose or broken alternator drive belt	Check alternator belt
	Headlight or bulbs burned out	Replace headlight or bulb
	Faulty switch or loose ground connection	Check switch and ground connection
	Blown fuse	Check fuse
	Faulty flashers	Check flashers

Step 6-1. Getting to a burned-out headlight.

Use a Phillips screwdriver to remove the trim. You should see additional screws behind the retaining ring. These screws adjust the headlight—don't disturb them. Hold the headlight with one hand and remove the retaining ring.

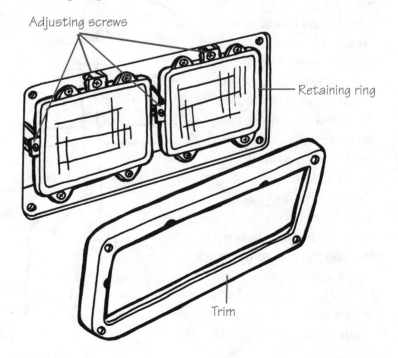

Adjusting screws

Retaining ring

Trim

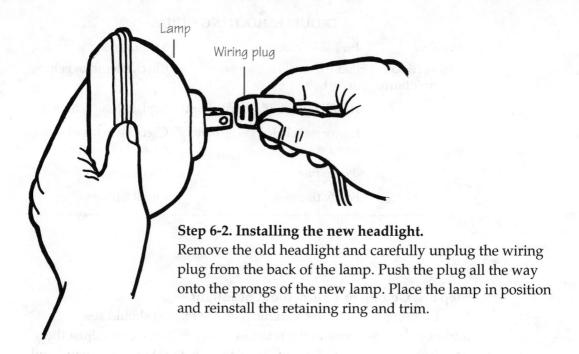

Lamp

Wiring plug

Step 6-2. Installing the new headlight.

Remove the old headlight and carefully unplug the wiring plug from the back of the lamp. Push the plug all the way onto the prongs of the new lamp. Place the lamp in position and reinstall the retaining ring and trim.

Step 6-3.
Aiming the headlights.

Headlights should be aimed professionally, but you can adjust them yourself if you accidentally moved the adjusting screws. First, make sure the car is on a level surface. Move the car so that the headlights are about a foot from a wall. Turn the lights on low beam. Use masking tape to mark a cross on the wall at the exact center of each beam. Now move the car straight back so that the headlights are about 25 feet from the wall.

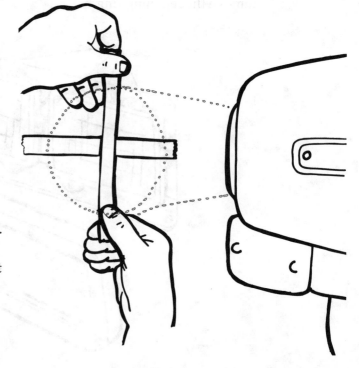

Step 6-4. Adjusting the headlights.

Use the adjusting screw at the top or bottom of each light to move the beam about 2 inches below the horizontal line in each cross. Now use the adjusting screw at the side of the left light to move the beam so that the center of the beam hits the vertical line of the left cross. Adjust the right light so that the center of its beam strikes about 2 inches to the right of the vertical line on the right cross. If your car has four headlights, adjust them all the same way. No separate adjustments are made for the high beams.

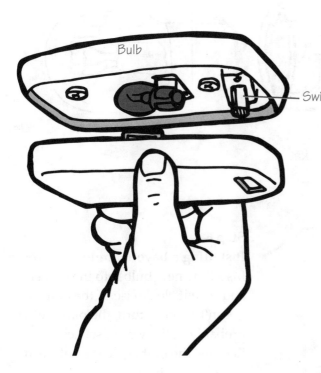

Step 6-5.
Getting to the dome, map, or makeup-mirror bulb.

If you don't see any screws around the light, squeeze the lens and snap it out. If you do see screws, remove them and take out the lens.

Step 6-6.
Replacing a dome, map,
or makeup-mirror bulb held by clips.
If the bulb is long and looks like a glass
fuse, carefully insert a small screwdriver
under one of the metal ends and pry it
from the clip. To install a new bulb, simply
press it between the two clips.

Step 6-7.
Removing a
standard bayonet bulb.
Press the bulb into the socket
and turn it counterclockwise
to free the pins. Remove
the old bulb and notice
the location of the pins
on each side of the base
of the bulb. If the pins are
not the same distance from the
bottom of the bulb, the bottom pin
must go into the bottom slot in the socket
to be reinstalled.

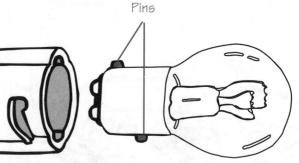

Pins

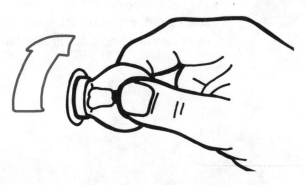

Step 6-8.
Installing a bayonet bulb.
Insert the new bulb into the socket
and turn it clockwise. If the bulb
doesn't want to turn, the pins are
probably in the wrong sockets.
Remove the bulb, give it a half turn
and reinstall it.

Brake, turn-signal, parking, and backup lights are usually mounted in the body of the car or in the front grill. If you can see screws holding the lens, the bulb can be replaced by removing the screws and lens. If no screws are visible, you'll have to reach the bulb from inside the trunk, behind the fender well, or inside the engine compartment.

Step 6-9.
Removing the lens from a brake,
turn-signal, parking, or backup light.
Remove the screws holding the retaining ring or the lens itself, and gently lift off the lens. Be careful not to tear the rubber gasket.

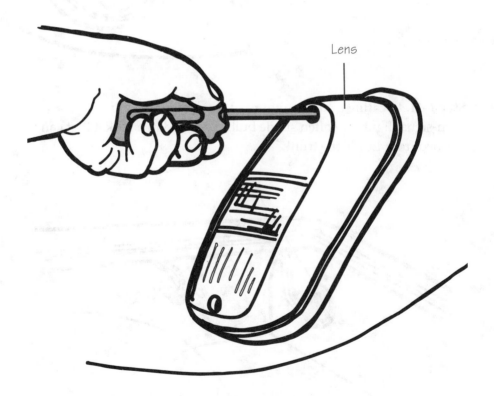

Lens

**Step 6-10.
Replacing a brake,
turn-signal, parking, or backup bulb.**
Remove the faulty bulb from the socket by
pushing in and turning the bulb a quarter-turn
counterclockwise. Install the new bulb by
aligning the pins with the proper slots in
the socket, then pressing the bulb in the
socket and turning it clockwise to
lock it in place.

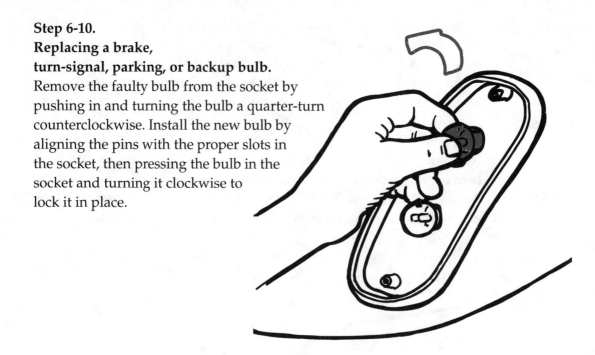

Step 6-11. Locating a socket-mounted (turn-signal) bulb.
Turn-signal lights are often single bulbs installed in a socket that can be
reached from inside the trunk.

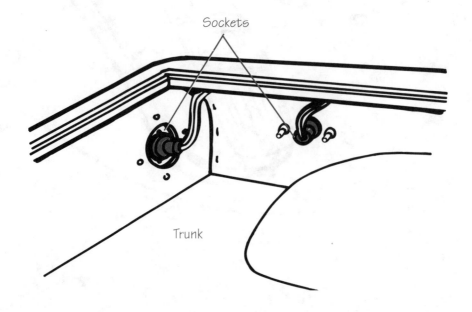

Shopping List for All Thumbs Guide to Car Care

- ☐ Battery hydrometer
- ☐ Coolant hydrometer
- ☐ Drain basin
- ☐ Droplight
- ☐ Emery cloth
- ☐ Fine sandpaper
- ☐ Fire extinguisher
- ☐ Funnel
- ☐ Fuse puller
- ☐ Jack
- ☐ Jack stands
- ☐ Jumper cables
- ☐ Lug wrench
- ☐ Needle-nose pliers
- ☐ Oil filter (strap) wrench
- ☐ Putty knife
- ☐ Rubber mallet
- ☐ Screwdrivers (Phillips and standard)
- ☐ Socket wrench
- ☐ Spark plug socket
- ☐ Terminal puller
- ☐ Tire pressure gauge
- ☐ Wheel blocks
- ☐ Wire battery brush
- ☐ Wire brush
- ☐ Wire feeler gauge
- ☐ Wrench (open-ended)
- ☐ _____
- ☐ _____
- ☐ _____

Battery hydrometer

Coolant hydrometer

Oil filter (strap) wrench

Fire extinguisher

Jumper cables

Wire feeler gauge

Needle-nose pliers

Putty knife

Standard screwdriver

Lug wrench

Phillips screwdriver

Socket wrench

Spark plug socket

Fuse puller

Wire battery brush

Terminal puller

Tire pressure gauge

Jack

Refer to the lists at the beginning of the chapters for the tools you need for individual projects.

Emergency kit

- ❏ Tire pressure gauge (for the glove box)
- ❏ Jumper cables
- ❏ Two screwdrivers
  (one standard and one Phillips)
- ❏ Adjustable wrench
- ❏ Pliers
- ❏ Flashlight (for the glove box)
- ❏ Roll of all-purpose wire

- ❏ Wheel chock
- ❏ ABC fire extinguisher
- ❏ A couple of clean rags
- ❏ Emergency flares
- ❏ First aid kit (sold preassembled)
- ❏ Pair of work gloves
- ❏ Duct tape
- ❏ _____

Safety tips

- ○ Have a first aid kit and an ABC-type fire extinguisher handy.
- ○ Never crawl under a car supported only by a jack.
- ○ Block the wheels when changing a tire.
- ○ Never completely remove a hot radiator cap.
- ○ Remove any jewelry (watches, bracelets, rings, long necklaces) before making repairs.
- ○ Don't wear loose clothing, ties, or scarves, and if you have long hair, tie it back out of the way.
- ○ Work slowly and carefully.
- ○ Read and understand all instructions.
- ○ Gather all your tools and required materials.
- ○ Work in a clean, well-ventilated area.
- ○ Have clean rags or paper towels handy.
- ○ Use the proper tools.
- ○ Use a droplight with a cage protecting the bulb.
- ○ Don't work on anything that is under warranty, or you could void the warranty.
- ○ For ambitious repairs, buy a service manual for your make of car at the parts department of your local dealer or auto parts house. You can also find repair manuals at most libraries. Don't attempt any repair unless you fully understand the job. Even professionals refer to service manuals at one time or another.
- ○ When in doubt, seek professional help.

From All Thumbs Guide to *Car Care* by Robert W. Wood.
© 1993 by TAB Books, a division of McGraw-Hill, Inc.

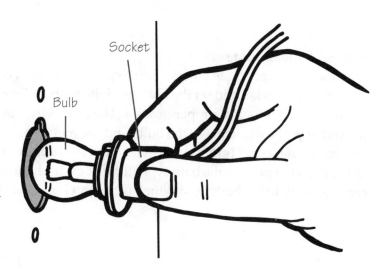

Step 6-12.
Removing the socket.
Turn the socket slightly,
about a quarter-turn
counterclockwise, and pull
it from the lens housing.
Replace the faulty bulb and
reinstall the socket.

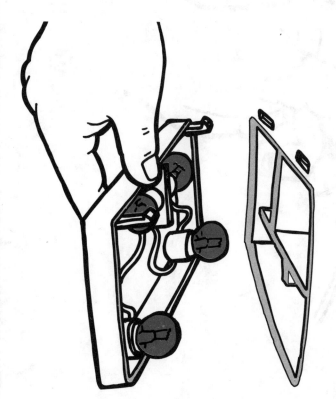

Step 6-13.
Replacing a bulb in a bulb housing.
Some lights have more than one bulb
mounted in a housing located inside
the trunk or engine compartment.
The housing often just snaps in place,
but it might be held by nuts. Remove
the housing and replace the faulty
bulb. Snap the housing back in place
or reinstall the nuts.

Step 6-14. Cleaning a socket.

Use fine sandpaper or an emery cloth to polish corroded contacts in the bottom of the socket and on the bottom of the bulb. Polish the inside of the socket to maintain a proper ground. The electricity travels through the contacts, the filaments in the bulb, and the metal base of the bulb to the side of the socket (ground), then through the frame of the car back to the negative post on the battery. Without a ground, the electricity can't get back to the battery, and the bulb won't burn.

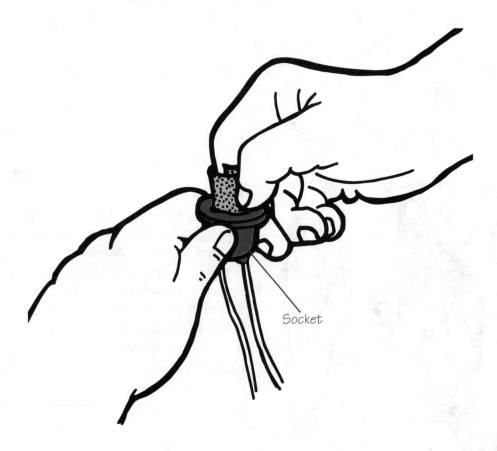

Socket

Step 6-15. Replacing a flasher.

Flashers seldom fail, so always check the lamp first. If the turn signals light but don't flash, or if none of the signal lights burn, you probably have a bad flasher. Flashers might be located near the firewall in the engine compartment, but they are usually just plugged into the fuse panel. Flashers can be metal or plastic, round or square. You should see two that are alike; one for turn signals and one for the hazard warning. To locate the flashers, turn on the ignition and the turn signals. Listen for a steady clicking. If you don't hear anything, turn on the hazard warning. When you find what you think is the flasher, place your hand on it. You should feel a vibration for each click. Check the flasher by swapping the one that clicks for the one that doesn't. Then simply unplug the faulty flasher and plug in a new one.

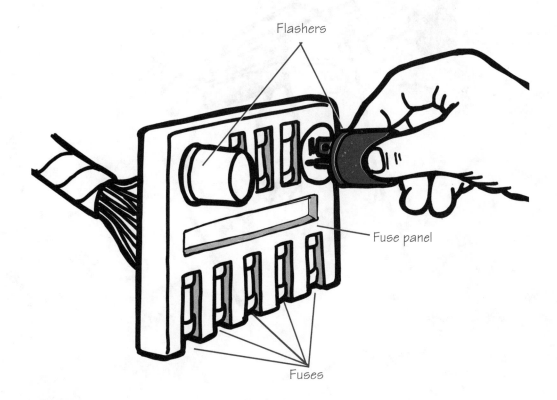

Step 6-16. Replacing a fuse.

Fuse panels are usually located in the glove compartment or on the driver's side beneath the instrument panel. Be sure to replace any fuse with a replacement of the correct size. Small, inexpensive plastic fuse pullers are available at any auto parts store. With the ignition off, fit the jaws of the puller over the bad fuse and pull it out. Press a new fuse with the same capacity into its place.

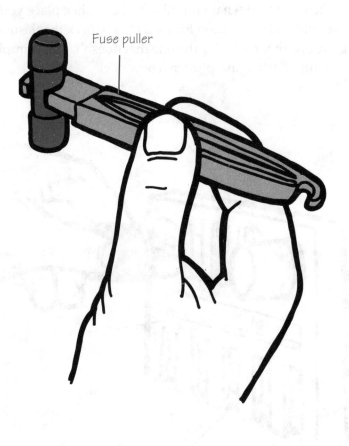

Fuse puller

CHAPTER SEVEN

Tires

Inspect your tires regularly for any excessive or unusual wear in the tread. Caring for tires is an easy and very important part of car maintenance. The way the tread wears indicates any problems with inflation or front-end alignment. The inspection can be made in three simple steps: First, kneel down and visually inspect all four tires. Then slowly run your hand over the tread to feel for any patterns of feathering (Step 7-5) or cupping (Step 7-7). Next, check the pressure in all four tires with a pressure gauge. Don't forget the spare tire. Make sure it's ready for use.

Know how to change a flat tire (Steps 7-10 through 7-17). When buying tires, shop around. The most expensive place to buy tires is probably at a new car dealership, followed by gas stations. Check the sports section of your local newspaper for specials. You'll probably find the best buys at independent tire dealers that carry several different brands.

Tools & Materials

- ❏ Pressure gauge
- ❏ Lincoln penny
- ❏ Wheel blocks
- ❏ Lug wrench
- ❏ Jack

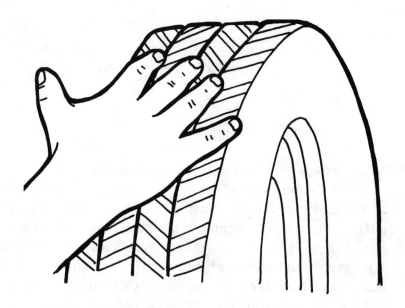

Run your hand over the tread to feel the tread pattern.

TROUBLESHOOTING GUIDE

Problem	Probable causes	Solutions
Tires not wearing evenly	Tire air pressure too high or too low	Check air pressure
	Wheels out of alignment	Have wheels aligne
	Defective suspension or steering	Have suspension ar steering checked
Tires vibrate or thump	Tires not balanced	Have tires balanced

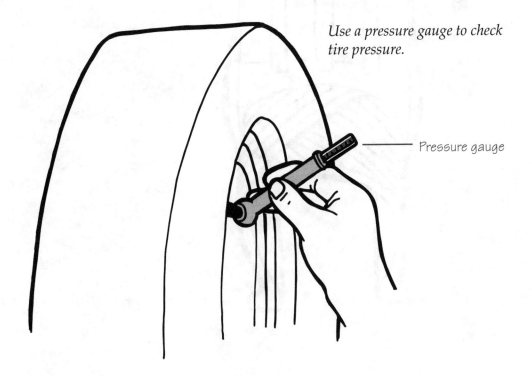

Use a pressure gauge to check tire pressure.

Pressure gauge

Step 7-1.

Knowing the type of tires on your car.

Three basic types of tires are on the market: bias, bias-belted, and radial tires. Bias tires have two or more crisscrossed layers of cords called plies. The more layers, the stronger the tire. Belted tires also have crisscrossed layers of cords, but they also have two or more fiberglass or steel belts bonded to the cord. Belted and bias tires can be put on the same car, but not on the same axle. Radial tires are the most popular type. They have layers of cords that run straight across at a right angle (radially) to the tread. Replace a radial tire only with another radial tire. Never mix other types of tires with radials.

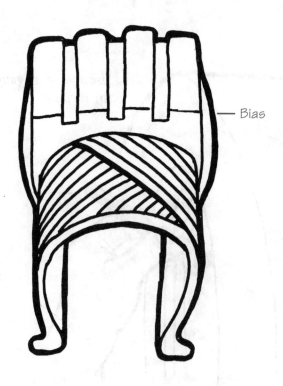
— Bias

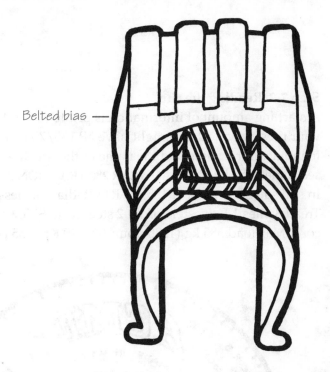

Belted bias

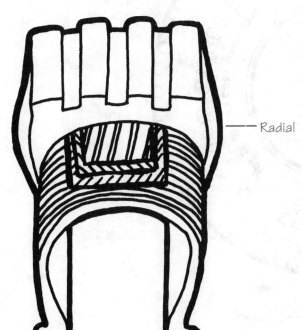

Radial

Step 7-2. Reading the tire.

A startling amount of information is printed in codes on the sidewall of your tires. A typical tire might have "P 185/75 R14" along with the manufacturer's name and the name of the tire. In smaller letters, you see something like "TREADWEAR 280 TRACTION A TEMPERATURE B." In still smaller letters: "P185/75 R14 Radial tubeless, Made in Canada, Tread 3 plies 1 Polyester cord + 2 steel cord, Sidewall 1 ply polyester cord, Max load 585 kg (1200 pounds), 240 Kpa (35 psi) Max press."

How the tire is used.

The P stands for passenger, the 185 indicates the width of the tire in millimeters, 75 is the ratio of the height to the width, and R14 indicates the radius of the wheel in inches.

How long the tire will last.

TREADWEAR 280 gives you an idea of how many miles you can expect from the tire. Each tire manufacturer assigns its own grading to its tires, so the number cannot be used to compare between brands. Check with your dealer for an explanation.

Tire traction.

Traction is graded A, B, or C. The traction grading tells you how well the tire stops on a wet surface. The tire graded A stops shorter on a wet road than a grade B or C.

Operating temperature of the tire.

Temperature is also graded A, B, or C. The tire graded A runs cooler and is less likely to fail at highway speeds than one graded B or C.

The maximum load and tire pressure.

The remainder of the printing tells you the maximum load of the tire, the maximum cold inflation pressure, the number of plies in the tread and sidewall, and where the tire was made.

Step 7-3. Checking the air pressure.

Check the air pressure before you start out, when the tires are cool. Never exceed the maximum inflation pressure printed on the side of the tire. The tire pressure recommended for your car is usually found in the glove box or in the owner's manual. Buy a pencil-type pressure gauge and leave it in the glove box. To check the pressure, unscrew the valve cap, fit the end of the gauge over the threaded end of the valve stem, and press in. If you hear any hissing, you don't have a good seal and the reading will not be accurate. When the air enters the gauge, a marked scale pops out of the gauge, displaying the pressure. If the pressure is too high, use the small stud on the gauge to press in the pin in the center of the valve stem. Bleed off a little air and check the pressure again. If the pressure is too low, drive to the nearest gas station and add air.

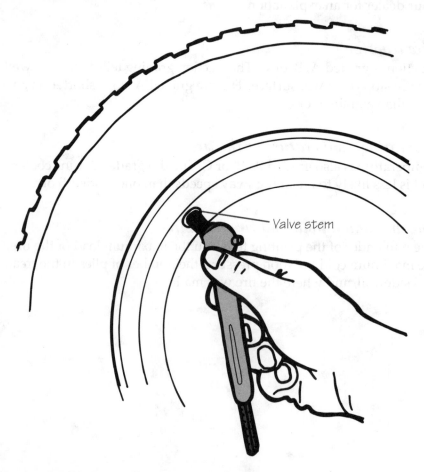

Valve stem

Step 7-4. Identifying tire wear caused by improper inflation.

Proper inflation is necessary to get the maximum performance from your tires. Underinflation causes premature wear at the outer edges of the tread. A low tire generates excessive heat, one of the biggest causes of wear and failure in tires. Overinflation causes excessive wear in the center of the tread. Because the center of the tread then carries most of the weight of the car, the tread is more apt to be damaged from potholes or objects in the road.

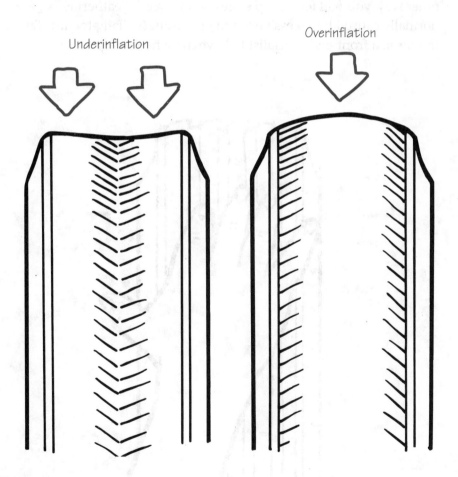

You can also identify tire wear caused by other problems. You should look for three basic wear patterns: feathering, wear along one side of the tread, and cupping.

Step 7-5. Checking for feathering.

To check for feathering, move the palm of your hand back and forth across the tread. Going one way, the tread will feel smooth; going the other way, you will feel sharp edges on the tread. Feathering is normally caused by excessive toe-in or toe-out (usually toe-in). Take the car to a front-end specialist to have the wheels aligned.

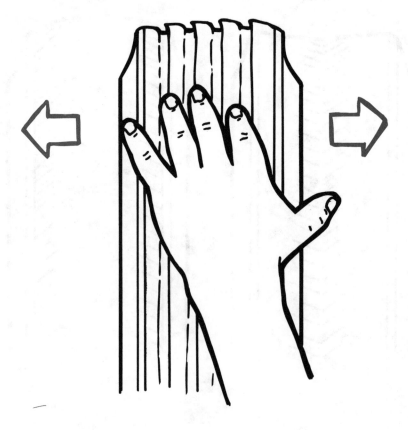

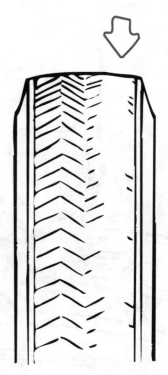

Step 7-6. Checking for wear on one side.
Wear along one side is caused by improper tilt of the
wheel in or out (camber). Have the wheels aligned.

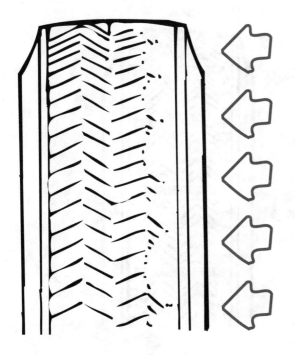

Step 7-7. Checking for cupping.
Cupping, or scalloped dips, along the
tread usually means you have worn
suspension parts (shock absorber, ball
joint, springs, etc.) or an unbalanced
wheel. Have the worn parts replaced
and the wheel balanced.

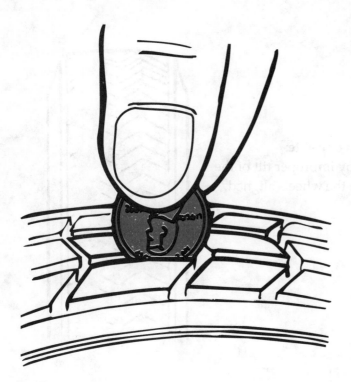

Step 7-8. Measuring the tread.
When the tread becomes worn down to 1/16 inch, driving on it is no longer safe and, in some states, is illegal. To check the depth of the tread, insert a penny upside down into a groove in the tread. If you can see all of Lincoln's head, you need new tires.

Step 7-9. Checking the wear bars.
Tires also have built in wear bars, which are small raised sections of rubber in the grooves that show you when the tires are worn out. When the tread is worn down to the same height as the wear bar, the bars appear as smooth bands about 1/2 inch wide across the tread. When these bands appear, you need a new tire.

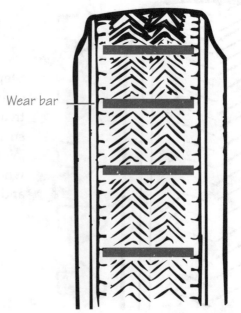

Wear bar

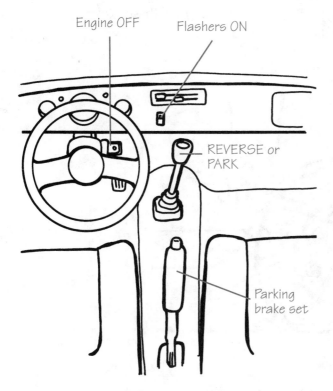

Engine OFF   Flashers ON

REVERSE or PARK

Parking brake set

Step 7-10. Changing a tire.
Pull off the road well away from traffic and park the car on level ground. Turn on the hazard lights and put the transmission in PARK, or in REVERSE for manual transmissions. Set the parking brake and turn off the engine. Check your owner's manual for details pertaining to your car. Remove the spare tire and jack.

Step 7-11. Blocking the tires.
Block the wheels at the end opposite of the flat tire to keep the car from rolling.

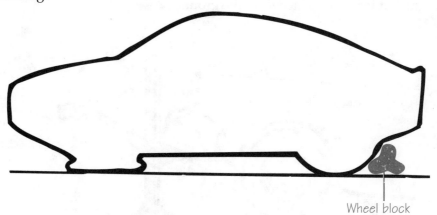

Wheel block

Step 7-12. Loosening the lug nuts.

Pry off the wheel cover and use the lug wrench to loosen each lug nut about one turn. Some lug nuts are marked with an "L." Turn these nuts clockwise to loosen. Unmarked nuts are loosened by turning counterclockwise.

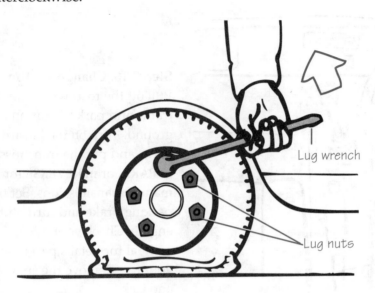

Lug wrench

Lug nuts

Step 7-13. Jacking the car.

Depending on the car, you either jack it from the bumper or from the side near the wheel. Check the instructions in your owner's manual. If the ground is soft, place a board under the base of the jack for extra support. Operate the jack slowly and smoothly. Raise the car so that the flat tire is at least 2 or 3 inches off the ground.

Jack

Board

Step 7-14.
Removing the flat tire.
Remove the lug nuts and place them in the wheel cover for safe
keeping. Then remove the flat tire.

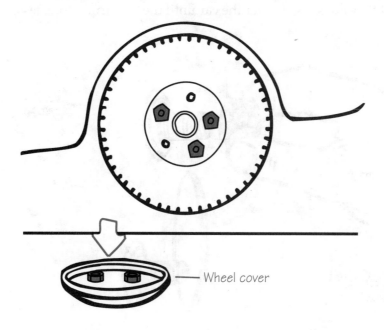

— Wheel cover

Step 7-15. Mounting the spare tire.
Supporting the spare tire with your
knee, lift it into position. Align the
holes in the wheel with the
mounting studs and push the tire
into place.

Mounting studs

Step 7-16. Installing the lug nuts.

Install the lug nuts with the tapered end pointing in. Tighten all of the nuts by hand; then tighten each one in a crisscross pattern with the lug wrench until they are snug. Lower the car until the tire firmly touches the ground.

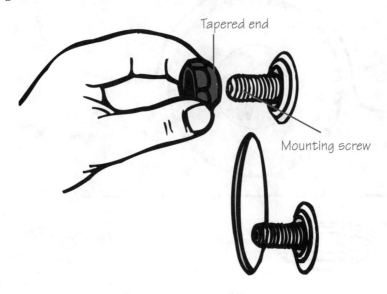

Tapered end

Mounting screw

Step 7-17. Completing the job.

Finish tightening the nuts as tight as you can in the same crisscross pattern. Lower the car the rest of the way. Tap the wheel cover in place with a rubber mallet or put it in the trunk to install later. Remove the wheel blocks. Put the flat tire and jack in the trunk and have the flat repaired or replaced as soon as possible.

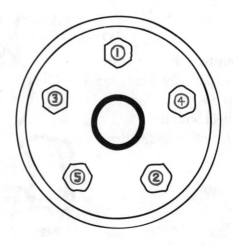

CHAPTER EIGHT

Air Conditioning

Your car's air conditioner consists of four basic parts: a belt-driven compressor powered by the car's engine; an expansion valve; the evaporator; and the condenser. The entire system is sealed and contains pressurized refrigerant. Because the system is sealed, any repair work should be left to a professional. Do not, for example, even attempt to tighten or loosen any fittings. The refrigerant is extremely cold. When exposed to air, it instantly freezes anything it contacts, including your skin or eyes. Although refrigerant is normally nontoxic, the gas becomes very poisonous, even fatal, if ignited. You can, however, take steps to make sure your air conditioner is working properly or determine when to have it serviced. Operate the air conditioner about once a week (even in the winter) to keep the internal parts lubricated.

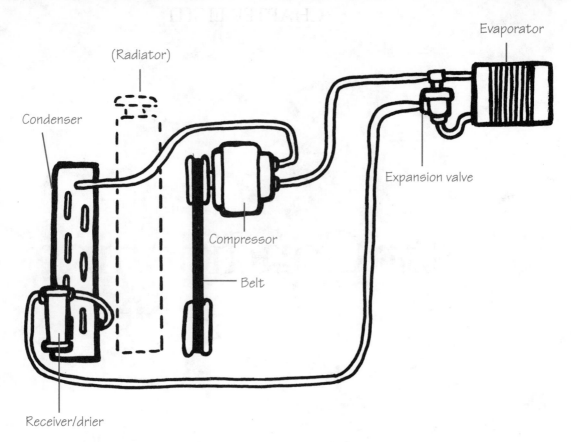

A typical air conditioning system.

TROUBLESHOOTING GUIDE

Problem	Probable causes	Solutions
Air conditioner does not blow air	Blown fuse	Check fuse
	Fan motor defective	Have fan motor replaced
Air conditioner does not blow cold air	Low refrigerant charge	Check refrigerant charge
	Broken or slipping compressor belt	Check compressor belt
	Magnetic clutch faulty	Check magnetic clutch

Tools & Materials

- ❏ Clean rag or paper towel
- ❏ Wrench
- ❏ Pry bar (or hammer handle)
- ❏ Garden hose
- ❏ Soft-bristled brush
- ❏ Needle-nose pliers

Step 8-1.
Checking the refrigerant level on a system with a sight glass.
Locate the receiver/drier. It is a metal cylinder, something like a small fire extinguisher, usually located in the front near the condenser.

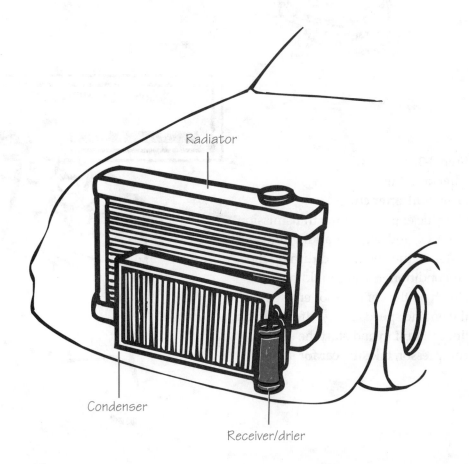

Radiator

Condenser

Receiver/drier

Sight glass

Receiver/drier

Step 8-2. Locating the sight glass.
The sight glass should be on top of
the receiver/drier, but it might be
in one of the metal lines going from
the receiver/drier. The sight glass
could have a protective cover made
of heavy paper. If so, remove the
cover. If not, wipe the sight clean
with a rag or paper towel.

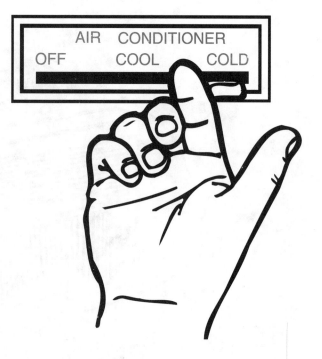

**Step 8-3.
Checking the
air-conditioner clutch.**
Start the engine, put the transmission
in PARK, and set the parking brake.
Listen to the engine and turn on the
air conditioner. You should hear the
clutch on the compressor engage and
the engine speed change. If the clutch
doesn't pull in and start the
compressor, take the car for service.

Step 8-4. Reading the sight glass.

With the air conditioner running, look through the sight glass. If it is clear and cold air is coming from the vents inside the car, the system is fully charged. If the sight glass is clear but the air from the vents is not cold, the system is empty. Take the car for service. If you see bubbles (be sure the clutch is still engaged), the system is low on refrigerant. If the sight glass is foamy, the system is very low and should be checked by a professional.

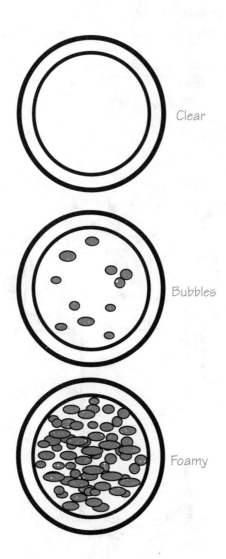

Clear

Bubbles

Foamy

Step 8-5.

Checking the level on a system without a sight glass.

With the engine running and the air conditioner on, locate the receiver/drier. You should see two metal lines coming from the top of the receiver/drier; one going toward the front to the condenser, and the other line going toward the back to the expansion valve. Place one hand on each line and compare the temperatures. If both lines are about the same temperature, the system is probably fully charged. If the line going toward the front and the condenser is much colder than the other line, the system is probably low on refrigerant. Have the system checked.

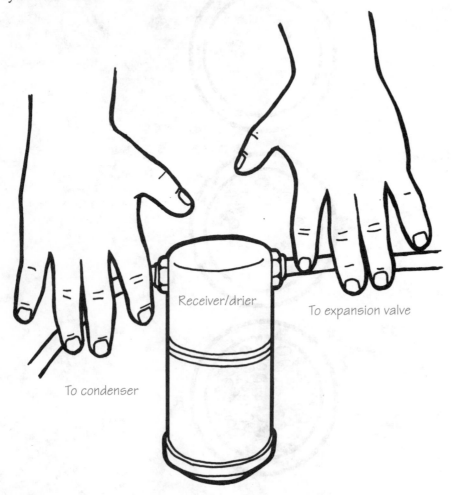

Receiver/drier

To expansion valve

To condenser

Step 8-6. Checking the compressor belt.
Examine the compressor belt for any cracks, fraying, or glazing caused by the belt slipping. If the belt has any damage, install a new one. Now start the engine and run the air conditioner for a few minutes to warm up the belt. Turn off the air conditioner and shut off the engine.

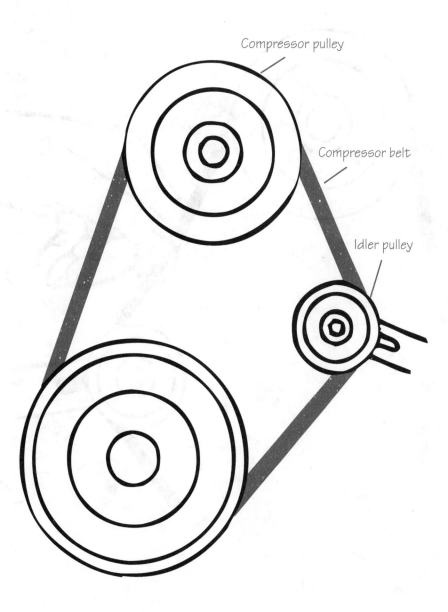

Compressor pulley

Compressor belt

Idler pulley

Step 8-7. Checking belt tension.

Check the tension of the belt by applying pressure with your thumb midway between the two pulleys. The belt should deflect no more than 1/2 inch, less if the belt is new.

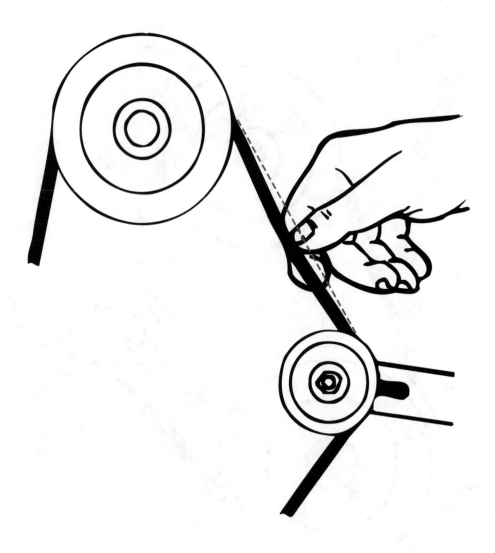

Step 8-8. Adjusting the compressor belt.

Examine the pulleys driven by the compressor belt. You should find one that has an adjustable slot. It could be the alternator pulley, an idler pulley, or the compressor pulley itself. If it is the compressor pulley, for example, use a wrench to loosen the mounting bolts. Place a pry bar (a hammer handle works fine) where you can use the leverage to shift the compressor out until the belt has the proper tension. Tighten the bolts while maintaining the tension on the belt. Remove the pry bar and recheck the belt's tension. Check the tension again after driving the car with the air conditioner running.

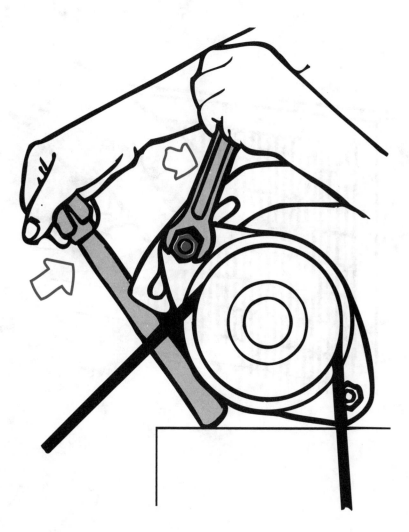

Step 8-9. Cleaning the condenser.

Because the condenser is in front of the radiator, it tends to collect bugs, leaves, and other debris. If you have enough room between the condenser and the radiator, use a garden hose to run a soft stream of water through the back of the condenser toward the front. If you have enough room between the grill and the front of the condenser, use a soft-bristled brush to remove any debris from the front of the condenser. Be careful not to bend any of the soft cooling fins. Carefully straighten any bent fins with needle-nose pliers.

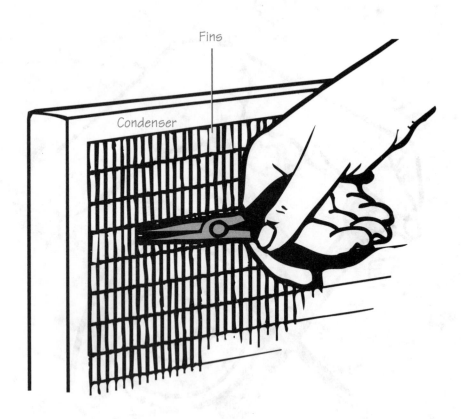

APPENDIX

General Troubleshooting Guide

Problem	Probable causes	Solutions
Exhaust smoke (blue)	Worn piston rings or valve seals	Take car for service
Exhaust smoke (black)	Rich air/fuel mixture	Have carburetor checked
	Stuck choke	Check position of choke
	Plugged air filter	Replace air filter
Car doesn't steer or ride well	Incorrect tire pressure	Check tire pressure
	Worn ball joints	Take car for service
	Loose or worn steering links	Take car for service
	Front end out of alignment	Take car for service
	No power steering fluid	Check power steering fluid
	Loose or worn power steering belt	Checking power steering belts
	Leaking power steering hose	Take car for service

Problem	Probable causes	Solutions
Car doesn't steer or ride well (Continued)	Power steering pump faulty	Take car for service
	Worn shock absorbers	Take car for service
	Worn springs	Take car for service
	Loose or broken sway bar	Take car for service
Car pulls to the right or left when you apply brakes	Uneven tire pressure	Check tire pressure
	Brake fluid or grease on brake linings	Take car for service
Brakes don't work	Brakes wet or overheated	Drive with slight pressure on brake petal to dry out brakes or stop and let the brakes cool
	Brakes wet or overheated	Drive with slight pressure on brake petal to dry out brakes or stop and let brakes cool
	Oily or glazed brake linings or pads	Take car for service
	Air in hydraulic brake system	Take car for service
	Leaky brake cylinder	Take car for service
	Broken brake line	Take car for service
Brakes fade when you apply pressure	Low brake fluid	Check brake fluid in master cylinder
	Brake self-adjuster faulty	Back car up and stop several times to adjust brakes
	Leak in hydraulic system	Check hydraulic system for leaks
	Air in hydraulic system	Take car for service
Alternator light comes on	Broken or slipping drive belt	Check drive belt

Problem	Probable causes	Solutions
	Faulty alternator or voltage regulator	Take car for service
Oil light comes on	Low oil level	Check oil level
	Clogged oil filter	Have oil and filter changed
	Faulty oil gauge	Take car for service
Temperature light comes on	Stop-and-go driving in hot weather	Stop car, raise hood, and allow engine to cool
	Low coolant level	Check coolant level
	Low engine oil	Check oil level
	Stuck thermostat	Check thermostat
Grinding noise from engine compartment	Faulty water pump	Take car for service
	Faulty alternator	Take car for service
	Faulty air conditioning compressor	Take car for service
Grinding noise at either front corner of car when car is moving	Faulty front wheel bearing	Take car for service
Grinding noise at either rear corner of car, when car is moving	Faulty rear wheel bearing	Take car for service
Grinding noise at any or all of the wheels when driving slow or applying brakes	Faulty brakes	Take car for service
A chirp or shrill whistle from the engine compartment	Slipping drive belt on power steering pump or air conditioner compressor	Check belts

Problem	Probable causes	Solutions
Exhaust odor in car	Leak in exhaust pipe	Have exhaust pipe checked
Gasoline odor in car	Leak in fuel line	Look for fuel leak and take car for service
Rotten-egg odor at tailpipe when engine is running	Excessive fuel reaching catalytic converter	Have fuel mixture adjusted Have catalytic converter replaced
Slightly sweet smell from engine compartment	Cooling system leaking	Check cooling system
Hot oily smell (sometimes with smoke from compartment) when the engine is warm	Oil leaking on hot engine	Check for oil leaks on engine then take car for service
Wet spot under the car		
Clear	Normal condensation from air conditioner	
Green or yellow	Coolant leak	Check coolant
Dark spot	Oil leaking from engine	Take car for service
Red spot	Transmission fluid leak	Take car for service

Glossary

ABC-type fire extinguisher
A multipurpose, dry-chemical fire extinguisher used to control paper, electrical, or fuel fires.

air filter   The device that traps dirt and dust to keep it from entering the carburetor.

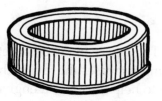

alternator   The device that operates electrical accessories and keeps the battery charged.

antifreeze   The common name for ethylene glycol, a chemical which, when mixed with water, is used as an engine coolant.

battery   The device that stores electrical energy.

carburetor   The device that vaporizes fuel and mixes it with air to form a combustible mixture.

choke   The device in the carburetor that reduces the air and increases the fuel in the air/fuel mixture to help start a cold engine.

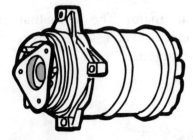

compressor   A device that increases the pressure, density, and temperature of a gas or liquid by forcing it into a smaller space.

condenser   The part of an air conditioning system, similar to a radiator, that cools the hot, high-pressure gas in the system.

crankshaft   The main rotating shaft in the engine that transmits power from the pistons to the transmission.

cylinder   A hole in the engine block in which a piston travels up and down.

dipstick   A metal rod used to measure the levels of oil, transmission fluid, and power steering fluid.

distributor   The part of the ignition system that distributes high voltage to each spark plug in sequence at the proper time.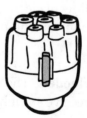

distributor cap   The cover on the distributor. The distributor cap has a tower for each plug wire and a center tower where the coil wire enters to carry electrical current to the rotor.

electrolyte The mixture of sulfuric acid and water that produces voltage and conducts electrical current in lead-acid batteries.

evaporator The part of the air conditioning system in which the refrigerant vaporizes into gas-absorbing heat and a fan blows cold air into the passenger compartment.

firewall The metal partition separating the passenger compartment from the engine compartment.

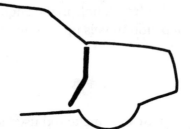

flasher A device that automatically interrupts the flow of electrical current, causing signal lights to blink on and off.

flooded The condition that occurs in the engine when the cylinders receive straight gas or a mixture of air and fuel that is too rich to burn.

fuel filter The device in the fuel line that removes dirt and other contaminants from the fuel before it enters the carburetor.

fuel pump   The mechanical or electrical device that transfers fuel from the fuel tank to the carburetor.

fuse   A safety device that protects an electrical circuit against overloads.

gasket   A layer of material placed between two surfaces to provide a tight seal.

ground   The return path in an electrical circuit, usually made up of the car frame and metal body parts.

hydrometer, battery   An instrument used to measure the specific gravity of electrolyte to determine the battery's charge state.

hydrometer, coolant   An instrument used to measure the ratio of antifreeze and water in the radiator.

jack   The device used to raise the car to change a tire.

jump-start Using a booster battery to start a car with a dead battery.

jumper cables Two color-coded cables used to conduct electricity from the working battery to the dead battery.

lug nuts The tapered metal nuts that fasten the wheels to the axle.

master cylinder The device in a hydraulic brake system that distributes hydraulic pressure to each wheel for braking.

PCV valve Positive crankcase ventilation valve. The PCV valve recycles exhaust gases back into the engine to be burned.

petcock The valve at the bottom of the radiator that drains the radiator.

piston   The movable part inside a cylinder that transmits power to the crankshaft.

post   The place where a cable is connected to the battery.

radiator   The device in the cooling system that removes heat from the coolant when air passes through it.

receiver/drier   The device in an air conditioning system that stores and removes moisture from the refrigerant.

rotor   The revolving part inside the distributor that conducts electricity to the individual spark plug wires.

thermostat   The temperature-sensitive device that opens or closes to regulate the coolant temperature in the cooling system.

transmission The system of gears that transfers power from the engine to the drive wheels.

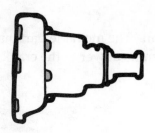

water pump The device that circulates coolant between the radiator and the engine.

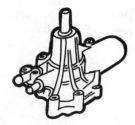

wire feeler gauge A set of round wires of precise diameters used to check the distance, or gap, between electrical contacts.

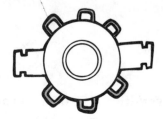

Index

A

acid buildup, neutralizing, 26
air cleaner, clogged, 49
air conditioner clutch, 108
air conditioning, 105-114
  basic parts, 105
  belt tension, 112
  checking clutch, 108
  compressor belt, 111-113
  condenser, cleaning, 114
  illustration, 106
  refrigerant level, checking, 107
  sight glass, 108-110
  tools and materials, 107
  troubleshooting guide, 106
air filter, 12-13
  checking, 13
  cleaning, 13
  removing, 12
air pressure, tires, checking, 96
alternator, loosening, 75
AMC, fuel filter, 56-57
antifreeze, correct amounts, 66

B

backup light, 83
basics, 1-18
  air filter, 12-13
  brake fluid, 11
  brakes, 6
  combustion chamber, 2
  coolant, 4
  cylinders, 2
  fuel pump, 3
  hydraulic fluid, 6
  master cylinder, 10
  oil, checking, 6-8
  pistons, 2
  power steering fluid, 11
  radiator, 5
  spark plugs, 2
  starter, 1
  tools and materials, 4
  transmission, 4
  transmission fluid, checking, 8-9
  water pump, 5
battery, 19
  checking, 21-34
    nonsealed battery, 22
    sealed battery, 21
    sight glass, 21
  clamp connection, 34
  cleaning, 25-27
    clamps, 27
    neutralizing acid buildup, 26
    posts, 27
    tray, 33
  disconnecting, 24-25
    clamp removal, 24

disconnecting *(continued)*
  installation, 33
  jump-starting, 29-31
  nonsealed, checking, 22
  old, removal, 32
  protecting the connections, 28
  reconnecting, 28
  replacement, 32-34
  sealed, 21
battery clamps, cleaning, 27
battery posts, cleaning, 27
bayonet bulb, 82
belted bias tires, 92-93
bias tires, 92
brakes, 6
  hydraulic fluid, 6

C

camber, 99
car won't start, 19-43
  battery, 19, 21-34
  choke, 39
  distributor cap and rotor, 35-38
  flooded engine, 39
  fuel pump, 19, 40-43
  tools and materials, 20
  troubleshooting guide, 20
changing oil, 14-18
changing tires, 101-104
  blocking tires, 101
  flat tire removal, 103
  jacking the car, 102
  job completion, 104
  lug nuts, installing, 104
  lug nuts, loosening, 102
  spare tire, mounting, 103
choke plate, 39
choke, sticking, 49
Chrysler, fuel filter, 56-57
combustion chamber, 2
compressor belt
  adjusting, 113
  air conditioning, 111
condenser, cleaning, 114
coolant, 4
cooling system, illustration, 59
cupping, 99
cylinders, 2

D

differential, 1
dipstick, 6-7
distributor cap and rotor, 35-38
distributor cap, 35-38
  checking inside, 36
  checking towers, 36
  removal, 35
  replacing, 38
dome light, 81-82
  bayonet bulb, removing, 82
  replacing bulb, 82

F

fan, 58
fan belt, 58, 74-77
  adjusting, 77
  checking, 74
  installation, 76
  loosening alternator, 75
  removal, 75
feathering, 98
flasher, 87-88
  replacement, 87
flat tire removal, 103
flooded engine, 39-40
Ford cars, fuel filter, 55
fuel filter, 53-57
  AMC, Chrysler, or import car, 56-57
  Ford car, 55
  General Motors cars, 53-54
fuel pump, 3, 40-43
  checking, 40
  disconnecting, 42
  installing, 43
  mounting, 43
  removing, 41
  removing old gasket, 42
fuse puller, 88

G

gap adjusting tool, 50
gasket, 42
General Motors cars, fuel filter, 53-54
glossary, 119-126

H

hose clamps, 68-69
  removal, 69
hoses, 58
hydraulic fluid, 6
hydrometer, 23, 67
  filling, 23
  reading, 23

I

ignition coil, 44
import car, fuel filter, 56-57

J

jacking the car, 102
jump-starting, 29-31
  black cable connection, 30
  ground connection, 31
  positive post identification, 29
  red cable connection, 30
  starting car, 31

L

lights, 78-88
  adjusting, 81
  aiming, 80
  brake, turn-signal, parking or
backup light, 83-88
  burned-out, getting to, 79
  dome light, 81-82
  fuse replacement, 88
  installation, 80
  tools and materials, 778
  troubleshooting guide, 79
lug nuts, 102-104
  installing, 104
  loosening, 102

M

makeup-mirror bulb, getting to, 81
master cylinder, 10-11
  adding brake fluid, 11
  removing cover, 10
mechanical fuel pump, 41, 43

N

neutralizing acid buildup, 26
nonsealed battery, 22-23
  hydrometer, filling, 23

O

oil changing, 14-18
  drain plug, removing, 16
  draining old oil, 16
  oil filter, 17
  raising car, 15
  refilling, 18
oil filter, 17
  installation, 17
  removing, 17
oil, 6-8, 14
  adding, 8
  changing, tools and materials, 14
  checking, 6-8, 6
  checking, dipstick, reading, 7
  dipstick, location, 6
overheating, 58-77
  coolant level, checking, 62
  fan belt, 74-77
  leaks, duct tape use, 61
  radiator cap removal, 61, 63
  radiator, 63-71
  radiator cap, checking, 63
  thermostat, 71-73
  tools and materials, 62
  troubleshooting guide, 62

P

parking light, 83
PCV valve, 49, 52
pistons, 2
power steering fluid, 11
pressure cap, 58

R

radial tires, 92-93
radiator, 5, 58, 63-71
  bent fitting, straightening, 70
  debris, cleaning, 67
  draining, 64

radiator *(continued)*
  filling, 66
  flushing system, 65
  hose removal, 69
  hose, installing new, 70
  hose clamps, removal, 68
  refilling, 71
  testing coolant, 67
radiator cap, 61-63
refrigerant level, checking, 107
rotor, 37
runs rough or dies, 44-57
  fuel filter, clogged, 53-57
  PCV valve, 52
  spark plug wires, 45-46
  spark plugs, 47-51
  tools and materials, 44
  troubleshooting guide, 45

S

sight glass, locating, 108
socket-mounted bulb, 84-86
  replacing bulb, 85
  socket cleaning, 86
  socket removal, 85
spare tire, 103
spark plug boot, 45
spark plug wires, 45-46
  checking, 45
  disconnection, 46
  numbering wires, 46
spark plugs, 2, 47-51
  black plugs, 48
  carbon on plugs, 49
  checking, 48-49
  gap, 50
  installing, 51
  oily plugs, 49
  removal, 47
  tightening, 51
spring clamp, 68
starter, 1

T

temperature light, 58
terminal pullers, 25

thermostat, 58, 71-73
  gasket, removal, 72
  housing, mounting, 73
  installation, 73
  removal, 72
  replacing, 71
tire pressure gauge, 91
tires, 89-104
  air pressure, checking, 96
  changing, 101-104
  feathering, 98
  improper inflation, 97
  maximum load, 94-95
  operating temperature, 95
  pressure, 95
    checking, 91
  reading, 94
  tools and materials, 90
  traction, 95
  tread measurement, 100
  tread pattern, 90
  troubleshooting guide, 91
  types, 92
  uses, 95
  wear bars, 100
  wear, 96-97
    cupping, 99
    improper inflation, 97
    side, 99
transmission, 4
transmission fluid, 8-9
  adding, 9
  checking, 8-9
  dipstick location, 9
  troubleshooting guide, 115-118
turn signal
  bulb replacement, 84
  removing lens, 83
  flasher, 87-88
twin-wire screw clamp, 68

W

water pump, 58
wear bars, tires, 100
wire feeler gauge, 50
wire spring clamp, 68
worm-gear clamp, 68
water pump, 5